This
book belongs to

_____

...a wife after
God's own heart.

A Wife After God's Own Heart

Elizabeth George

HARVEST HOUSE PUBLISHERS

EUGENE, OREGON

Cover by Garborg Design Works, Minneapolis, Minnesota

Cover photo © Denis Boissavy/Getty Images

A WIFE AFTER GOD'S OWN HEART
Copyright © 2004 by Elizabeth George
Published by Harvest House Publishers
Eugene, Oregon 97402
www.harvesthousepublishers.com

Library of Congress Cataloging-in-Publication Data

George, Elizabeth, 1944-
  A wife after God's own heart / Elizabeth George.
     p. cm.
Includes bibliographical references.
  ISBN-13: 978-0-7369-1167-2 (pbk.)
  ISBN-10: 0-7369-1167-7 (pbk.)

  1. Wives—Religious life. 2. Christian women—Religious life. 3. Marriage—Religious aspects—Christianity. I. Title.
  BV4528.15.G46 2004
  248.8'435—dc22   2003018696

Printed in the United States of America

07 08 09 10 11 12 /BP-KB/ 10 9

For Jim—
Thank you for being
a husband after God's own heart
so that I could grow into
a wife after God's own heart!

Acknowledgments

As always, thank you to my dear husband, Jim George, M.Div., Th.M., for your able assistance, guidance, suggestions, and loving encouragement on this project.

About the Author

Elizabeth George is a bestselling author and speaker whose passion is to teach the Bible in a way that changes women's lives. For information about Elizabeth's books or speaking ministry, to sign up for her mailings, or to share how God has used this book in your life, please write to Elizabeth at:

Jim and Elizabeth George Ministries
P.O. Box 2879
Belfair, WA 98528

Toll-free fax/phone: 1-800-542-4611
www.ElizabethGeorge.com
www.JimGeorge.com

～

Contents

Becoming...

A Wife After God's Own Heart

A wife after God's own heart. What wife wouldn't want to be this? And what wife doesn't yearn for a happy marriage that is satisfying and exciting? If you are like most women (and like me!), you can always use a little help, motivation, and wisdom for improving and refreshing your relationship with your husband. To help make your desires for your marriage a reality, I've written this honest and helpful book—after 38 years of marriage—to share what I've learned along the way about building a better marriage, a marriage after God's own heart! This instructive and encouraging book...

> ...covers *12 areas of your life as a wife*—What the Bible says about the areas that really matter to the health and vibrancy of your marriage.

> ...includes *a list of "little things" that make a big difference in your marriage* at the end of each chapter. These "little things" are designed to stimulate and guide you to work out the many "little" ways you can practically fulfill your role as a wife.

I've also written a companion volume—*A Wife After God's Own Heart Growth and Study Guide*—just for you. This companion volume will further embed God's desires for you as a wife into your heart and daily life. As you work through the practical insights, scriptures, and helpful hints included in this wonderful growth guide, you'll find your heart—and your marriage!—being miraculously transformed. Don't miss out on taking this additional step to becoming a wife after God's own heart! You'll be glad you did...and so will your husband!

Join me now on a journey down the path of comprehending and implementing God's desires for us as His wives. And to make this journey even more enjoyable, ask your husband to join you by reading the companion book, *A Husband After God's Own Heart,* by Jim George.

Dear friend, no matter what your age or what state your marriage is in today, and regardless of what season of marriage you and your husband have entered, *A Wife After God's Own Heart* is for you. It presents God's timeless guidelines for you as a wife. As you'll hear me say throughout the book and in each of the 12 areas of your marriage, *God's Word works!*

So read on! Explore with me what God, the Creator of marriage, has to say about your relationship with your husband. And share your journey with others. With this book in hand, you can...

...read it before you marry

...read it alone to enhance your marriage

...read it together with your husband

...read it along with a friend or small reading group

...read it in a women's or couples' Bible study

...read it in your women's Sunday school class

...read it in your couples' Sunday school class

May God richly bless you as you continue growing in Him, growing in your faith in Him, and growing in your understanding of His plan for you as a wife after His own heart!

1

Growing in the Lord

*Seek first the kingdom of God and His righteousness,
and all these things shall be added to you.*
MATTHEW 6:33

Whenever I think about the first 30 years of my life, I automatically think, *That's when I did everything wrong!*

Why would I say this?

Because, my new reading friend, that's when there was no rhyme or reason for my life. That's when there were no guidelines for my life, no instructions for how to live my life. That's when I wanted what I wanted and did things my way. In short, that's when I did not have a relationship with God...which is why I am choosing to begin our book here, with God as the Number One way to make a difference in your life and in your marriage.

And what was it that I wanted for those three difficult decades? I wanted a lot of things, and most of them were things that every person wants. My personal "I Want" list included happiness, fulfillment, a life of meaning and contribution. I don't remember wanting fame or fortune, or to climb any corporate ladders or shatter any glass ceilings. No, I wanted what I'm sure you also want—a life that matters and counts. I dreamed of a life of joy and graciousness. And thrown into my dreams was, of course, a happy marriage that was satisfying and exciting.

I did marry at age 20, as I was beginning my senior year of college. Jim was 22 and entering his senior and fifth year in pharmacy school. There was the usual stir and flutter and frenzy of emotions that accompanies every new budding love relationship. Ours was truly love at first sight as we passed and smiled at each other regularly on our way to and from classes. Then came the "blind date" in November...with a proposal for marriage on Valentine's Day...and the wedding on June 1. Wow, what a whirlwind of excitement!

Things went well for a while. And then... Well, both Jim and I would tell you that after eight years, things became awfully empty and got pretty rocky, even after two children were added to the makeup of the George family.

Then a "miracle" occurred, and we became a *Christian* family. By God's grace, our hearts were opened to the truth of Christ...and by God's grace, we responded to that truth. And, beloved, that has made all the difference in the world! Things have never been the same. Before becoming Christians, we were like a couple with a great car...only we had no key. We couldn't get the car started. We couldn't make it work. We couldn't use it. We couldn't go anywhere.

My friend, a relationship with God *is* the key, the key to all of life, including your marriage. And that's what this chapter is all about—growing in the Lord. And that means learning what God, the Creator of all things *and* of marriage, has to say. You see, God and God alone possesses the instruction book for your marriage, and He's made it available to you. He knows what makes a marriage work. And He's written His divine guidelines right in the Bible. We'll look at what God has to say to you and me as wives in the chapters to come, but for now, let's see why it's important for you as a wife to grow in the Lord.

First Things First

I've chosen as our theme verse for this chapter a beloved favorite of many Christians. They are the words—and the heart!—of Jesus. They were spoken to His disciples and His followers. And they address the concerns of daily life. After telling His listeners not to worry, Jesus said they should instead "seek first the kingdom of God and His righteousness, and all these things shall be added to you" (Matthew 6:33).

Now, how does Jesus' teaching apply to you and me as wives? Well, married or single, *every* Christian is to put first things first. *Every* Christian is to seek the Lord first and foremost. God expects *every* Christian to grow. For instance...

☞ The apostle Peter wrote that we are to "grow in the grace and knowledge of our Lord and Savior Jesus Christ" (2 Peter 3:18).

☞　He also urged you and me to, "as newborn babes, desire the pure milk of the word, that you may *grow* thereby" (1 Peter 2:2).

☞　And the writer of Hebrews, in Chapter 5, chastised his readers with this scathing rebuke: "By this time you ought to be teachers, [but] you need someone to teach you again the first principles of the oracles of God; and you have come to need milk and not solid food. For everyone who partakes only of milk...is a babe" (verses 12-13). In other words, these people had not grown.

So how do we grow in the Lord? Answer: By putting God first. That's how spiritual growth occurs. And the most tried-and-true way to put God first is to read His Word, the Bible, and obey it. I like to think of spiritual growth as a three-step process. Keep in mind as you note them that all three steps are absolutely necessary to grow in the Lord. There are no shortcuts to spiritual growth.

Step #1—*Discover* through reading the Bible what God says about your life and how He wants you to live it. How is this done? By listening to God's heart through His Word. By reading and paying attention to the teachings in the Bible. By learning more about Him and His standards for righteousness.

Step #2—*Discern* through studying the Bible the meaning and implications of what you are reading. This is the point where you pray and seek to understand what God has said in the Bible.

Step #3—*Do* through heartfelt obedience what you have read and learned, discovered and discerned. This is the step where you do something about what you now know to be the will of God. This is where you put your knowledge into action in your life.

How's Your Heart?

Now, here's a question for you: How's your heart? Is your heart strong in faith...or weak? Is it a hot heart...or perhaps one that's losing its fire? A woman—and a wife—after God's own heart is someone who follows hard after Him and close behind Him (see Psalm 63:8). Therefore prayer and awareness of weak—or sinful—areas in your walk with God can be the beginning of even greater growth. God desires that we develop spiritual muscle so we are strong enough to stand against the powers of this world and to resist its pressures. God asks that you and I "do not conform any longer to the pattern of this world, but be transformed by the renewing of your mind" (Romans 12:2).

> *God desires that we develop spiritual muscle so we are strong enough to be His kind of wife.*

Here's another question for you: Are you satisfied with your current condition, spiritual maturity, and rate of growth? If so, you will grow no more. However, if there is a holy desire to grow in the Lord, to know God in a deeper, more intimate way, to be a woman after *His* heart, to strive toward His standards, to please Him, to be more Christlike, to identify, attack, and triumph over ungodly conduct and practices...then yours is the soft, responsive-to-God heart that will grow in the Lord.

Deciding to Grow

I'm sure you are as busy as I am. Honestly, every morning when I wake up, I wonder if I am going to make it through the day in front of me—if I'm going to get everything done, if I'll have the time and energy it will require to take care of my responsibilities at home and to others. Then one day it hit me that *I* sit in the driver's seat concerning most of the structure of my every day, including growing in the Lord. *I* decide whether the things of the Lord are really that important to me...or not. *I* decide whether I will make the effort to grow...or not. *I* decide whether I will schedule in the time it takes to grow, to meet with God regularly, to stop, look, and listen to Him by reading my Bible...or not.

> *The most important thing you must decide to do each and every day as a wife is to put the Lord first.*

So, dear one, as you can see, you and I are our own best ally...or our worst enemy, depending upon our choices concerning spiritual growth. I remember the day some months after becoming a Christian that I wrote an impassioned letter to God about the issues in my life at that time. It was sort of my covenant with Him to seek to grow—my commitment to grow in Him. It expressed the desires of my heart to mature as a Christian, along with my dreams of honoring and serving Him. I included the issues and areas in my life as a wife and mother that definitely fell under the "Needs Improvement" column. And I included the practices in my life that I labeled "Sin Areas," purposing to be done with them. I prayed on paper that God, through His great grace, would come to my aid and sustain my deepest desires to grow.

I saved the spiral stenographer's pad where I wrote my "Letter of Commitment" to God those many years ago. It has aged (about 30 years worth!), and how I thank God it was written in ink and not pencil! And now I want to ask two things of *you*. First, realize that this is the *commitment* section of this chapter. A section like this will occur throughout the book that asks you (and me!) to determine to grow, to determine to move out, to determine to take action, to determine to do the "putting off and putting on" of the practices and attitudes God calls us to, to determine to pay the price to follow after God—to put Him first, whatever that cost may be and however high it may soar, no matter what. I know my heart is racing right this minute as I'm writing about the most important thing you and I must decide to do each and every day of our lives—to put first things first and make the choices that can help us grow in the Lord.

Second, I want you to write out in your own way, in your own words, and from your own heart, your personal commitment to God. Make a commitment—a decision—

and determine to grow into the woman—and wife—you yearn to be—a woman after God's own heart, one who will do all *His* will (Acts 13:22). You'll be glad you did! And by the way, save it in a special place and read it often.

Tending Your Growth

Just as any skill or talent requires careful attention, so does your precious, priceless spiritual growth. What will it require?

Spiritual growth results from discipline. Winning a race requires purpose and discipline. Paul uses this illustration to explain that the Christian life takes hard work, self-denial, and grueling preparation. As Christians, we are running toward our heavenly reward. The essential disciplines of prayer, Bible study, and worship equip us to run with vigor and stamina. Don't merely observe from the grandstand; don't just turn out to jog a couple of laps each morning. Train diligently—your spiritual progress depends upon it.

Spiritual growth results from self-denial. At times we must give up something good in order to do what God wants. Each person's special duties determine the discipline and denial that he or she must accept. Without a goal, discipline is nothing but self-punishment. With the goal of pleasing God, our denial seems like nothing compared to the eternal, imperishable reward that will be ours.[1]

My dear friend, your "special duties" as a wife definitely require discipline and denial. And your *reward* for faithfully tending your growth? How about a gentle and quiet spirit that is precious in God's sight (1 Peter 3:4)? How about bringing honor to God as you live out His Word and His will for wives (see Titus 2:5)?

Reaping God's Blessings

Oops! I almost got ahead of myself. This is the *blessings* section, but I just had to mention those two spiritual growth truths. But let's go on and count—and consider—a few more blessings you will reap as you grow in the Lord. As you tend to your growth you'll find...

Your behavior changes. How? You will take on more of the character of Christ. You'll become more Christlike as God's Word and your walk of obedience work together to conform you to His image (Romans 8:29). In short, your life will be changed.

Your relationship with your husband changes. (And, by the way, this goes for your relationships with *all* people!) As your behavior changes (for the better, of course), and as you put more and more godly practices into place and heed more and more of God's commands, and as you grow in the Lord, you'll be a better wife. You'll manifest more of God's love, peace, patience, kindness, and goodness. You'll display more of a spirit of meekness and gentleness, not to mention greater self-control (Galatians 5:22-23). Now I ask you, why wouldn't these spiritual changes make a difference and bless you and others, beginning with your closest, most intimate relationship—your husband? They do...and they will!

And think of the difference such glorious changes will make in your dear husband's life. He'll be more relaxed... instead of waiting for the next blow-up or attack. He'll be more comfortable with you, knowing the two of you can communicate peacefully. He'll be more appreciative of you as a wife as he senses your heartfelt concern and support of his endeavors. He might even talk to you more often and about deeper subjects (like the issues and challenges on his job), knowing he has a tender, sensitive, sympathetic, and wise listener to share them with, knowing he has a wife who will pray for him.

You are blessed. Growth is definitely rewarding. You'll experience unspeakable rewards as you surprise yourself by the way you handle life's challenges and difficulties, as you marvel at your peace of mind, as you (miracle of miracles!) hear yourself speaking with wisdom and expressing comfort and encouragement to your dear husband. Oh, you will most definitely be blessed! And when the rewards and blessings tumble in, there is only one response to make and one person to thank—and that is the response of thanksgiving and gratitude to *God* for His marvelous grace!

Heart Response

On one very special evening, Jim and I had the opportunity to dine with the founder of Harvest House Publishers.

As we asked questions of this legendary man and he shared openly, he made a statement I'll never forget. He said, "Three words will sell a book—*simple, love,* and *home.*"

My precious reading friend, I'm not selling anything, but here's how I'm thinking after reading what I've shared in this opening chapter. Growing in the Lord is *simple!* There is nothing new or earth-shattering here. Life-changing, yes, but you probably already know these simple (there's that word again!), foundational guidelines to spiritual growth. Like the cookbooks I received at my bridal shower, they were simple, basic, fundamental—the first-steps and the how-tos of cooking. As simple as simple can be. Aren't you thankful that God keeps it simple when it comes to such a mystical, mysterious element as spiritual growth? We only need to know what God says is the basic recipe for being a woman and a wife after His own heart...and to faithfully follow His recipe. That's what "great creations" are made up of. And I'm praying that you and I will become just such creations as we faithfully follow these very few-but-simple steps for growing in the Lord!

Little Things That Make a Big Difference

1. Read your Bible every day.

Keep in mind that something is better than nothing, so aim for at least five minutes a day of Bible reading. That's about how long it takes to read one chapter in your Bible. Because of the subject matter of this book, and especially that of the next chapter, I suggest this schedule for your first five days:

Day 1 . . . . . . Genesis 1
Day 2 . . . . . . Genesis 2
Day 3 . . . . . . Genesis 3
Day 4 . . . . . . Ephesians 5
Day 5 . . . . . . Colossians 3

Then go back and begin at Genesis 4 and finish the book of Genesis one day at a time, one chapter at a time.

2. Pray for your husband three times every day.

Pray before he wakes up, at noon, and right before he comes home from work. Of course it will be easy to repeat this exercise every day for a week. Then, of course, you'll want to do it for life!

3. Plan to go to church this week.

Whether you are a little rusty on your church attendance, haven't been going at all, or don't know where to go, planning to attend this week will set your personal church wheels in motion. Place this all-important "date" on your calendar. Then make any necessary phone calls to neighborhood churches or friends to find out where to go, the exact times of the weekly services, and any other information you might need regarding a couples' class or a program for your children. Then begin the night before to get your act together—lay out your Bible, organize for a no-hassle breakfast, and get to bed a little early.

It's important that you talk to your husband about your desire to go to church. Ask him if he would like to go along with you and see what it's like. Tell him you value his opinions. Also share the information you've gathered and ask for his input. If he doesn't want to go to church with you, that's okay. Your assignment is to be friendly, excited, and to make a move in the direction of attending church yourself. God's job is to work on your husband's heart. And, of course, you'll be praying for him!

4. Sign up for a Bible class or Bible study.

I know you're busy, but you should never be too busy to take care of your spiritual growth. This "little" exercise may require making a few phone calls, but it will be worth it when you experience the exhilarating joy of growing in the Lord, which is the most important way to make a big difference in your life and your marriage!

5. **Purchase or borrow a Christian book on any topic.**

Ask your friends and other Christians for their favorite Christian book titles. You can't buy every book, but you can create a list to remind you which ones to purchase in the future. And don't forget to make good use of your church library. It's been said that "by spending 15 minutes a day you can read 25 books in a year."[2] Now, can't you scrape up 15 minutes today...and every day? As you learn from authors and teachers and scholars who share their knowledge and their passion for God and His Son, you, too, will grow in knowledge!

6. **Write a letter of commitment to God.**

On paper, pour out your desire to grow spiritually. It will only take you about five minutes...but those few minutes could set in motion the direction for the rest of your life!

2

*W*orking *as* a *T*eam

Two are better than one,
because they have a good reward for their labor.
ECCLESIASTES 4:9

*A*s I shared in the previous chapter, I lived....no, I *survived* 30 years of life without any guidelines. Then, as a new Christian who had failed miserably as a wife for eight years, I wanted to know exactly what it was that God wanted me to know, be, and do. I was a new creature in Christ, and I wanted to find out the "new" way—God's way—of being a wife. So I dug into my Bible (which was also new!) to find out what it said about my role as a wife. Briefly, here's what I found regarding the roles for both husband and wife, which together make up God's winning combination. As you read, I think you'll notice that God's plan is quite simple.

God's Winning Combination

As you read through these guidelines from the Bible, please invite God to open your heart to His instructions and His plan for your life as a wife. And by all means, hang in there. These are God's foundational laws for your marriage, and they never have changed...and they never will. Here we go!

A husband is to lead in his marriage and family. In the most basic terms, when God created the first husband–wife team, the man and woman were told as a couple to "be fruitful and multiply; fill the earth and subdue it" (Genesis 1:28). However, after their fall into sin, things changed. God then said to the woman in Genesis 3:16, "Your desire shall be for your husband, and he shall rule over you" (or "be your master"—TLB).

Later, in the New Testament, God repeated this guideline: "Wives, submit to your own husbands, as to the Lord. For the husband is head of the wife....Therefore, just as the church is subject to Christ, so let the wives be to their own husbands in everything" (Ephesians 5:22-24). Also, "wives, submit to your own husbands, as is fitting in the Lord" (Colossians 3:18). This means that in the same way you and I submit to the Lord, we are to also willingly follow our husband's leadership.

(*A thought:* Don't you think it's interesting to note that God did not tell husbands to *lead?* No, His communication was with us as wives, letting us know that we should *follow* our husband's leadership.)

A husband is to work and to provide for his wife. Things began well in the Garden of Eden, with man and woman as the inhabitants of a perfect environment. But, my friend, they certainly did not end well! After God's first couple disobeyed Him, He said to the man, "In toil you shall eat of [the ground] all the days of your life....In the sweat of your face you shall eat bread" (Genesis 3:17,19). As a result of the curse God placed upon the soil after Adam and Eve rebelled against Him, men would struggle to extract a living from the soil. In other words, all their lives men would have to work and labor and "sweat" so they and their families could eat and live.

A husband is to love his wife. This guideline is seen in several different scriptures. "Husbands, love your wives, just as Christ also loved the church and gave Himself for her" (Ephesians 5:25). "So husbands ought to love their own wives as their own bodies; he who loves his wife loves himself" (verse 28). "Husbands, love your wives and do not be bitter toward them" (Colossians 3:19). "Husbands... dwell with them with understanding, giving honor to the wife, as to the weaker vessel" (1 Peter 3:7).

These teachings mean that a Christian husband is to show the same kind of love toward his wife as Christ showed to the church when He died for her. A husband is also to treat his wife with tender loving care, caring for her in the same meticulous way he cares for his own body. In addition, a husband is to be kind to his wife, being thoughtful and considerate of her needs as "the weaker sex," and watching out for bitterness and harshness.

A wife is to help her husband. In fact, we might say this is why God created a wife for Adam, the first man.

When God surveyed His remarkable handiwork on Day Six of Creation, one more thing was needed. As the Bible reports, "Adam gave names to all cattle, to the birds of the air, and to every beast of the field. But for Adam there was not found a helper comparable to him" (Genesis 2:20). "And the LORD God said, 'It is not good that man should be alone; I will make him a helper comparable to him'" (verse 18). In other words, man needed someone "who could share man's responsibilities, respond to his nature with understanding and love, and whole-heartedly cooperate with him in working out the plan of God."[1] The result was Eve, the first woman and the first wife. *She* was the helper God created for Adam. *She* was God's solution to man's need for a helper and a companion. *Together* they were perfectly complete.

A wife is to submit to her husband. This makes sense after learning that the husband is to lead in the marriage. If someone (God says the husband) is to lead, then someone (God says the wife) must follow. To repeat a bit, here's how God expresses it: "Wives, submit to your own husbands, as to the Lord...as is fitting in the Lord....Be submissive to your own husbands."[2] This means wives must adapt themselves to their husbands' leadership and their way of leading.

A wife is to respect her husband. God instructs, "Let the wife see that she respects her husband" (Ephesians 5:33). A Christian wife is to "reverence" and respect, praise, and honor her husband. And finally...

A wife is to love her husband. Here's where the fun begins! Married women are "to love their husbands" (Titus 2:4). In other words, we are to be affectionate and treat our husbands in a loving manner—to cherish and enjoy our husbands as a best friend!

What a winning combination! The husband leads, loves, and works hard to provide, while the wife follows, loves, helps, and appreciates his efforts.

Following God's Plan

Do you know how some wives follow God's plan? They become husband-watchers. You see, they know what God says their husbands are supposed to do and be. They know how their husbands are supposed to treat them. And instead of taking care of their own faithfulness to their God-given assignment as wives, they take on the self-appointed role of playing "Holy Spirit" in their husbands' lives, pointing out their faults and shortcomings. These wives may even assume a "when...then" attitude. In their hearts (and maybe even verbally), they say, "*When* he does this or that, *then* I'll do this or that." They postpone obedience to their roles as wives and make it conditional to that of their husbands'.

But I am sharing both the husband's and the wife's roles in this chapter for two reasons. First, you and I should know what the Bible teaches about marriage. And second, if we are aware of our husbands' roles and responsibilities, we can be more understanding of the pressures on them and become better "helpers." I in no way mean for you to keep records concerning your spouse's behavior or to "grade" him as a husband. (That wouldn't be very "respectful," would it?) And I certainly don't intend for any woman to postpone obedience to God's clear communication to her as a wife while waiting on her husband to change...or grow...or move out in action...or become a contender for the "Husband of the Year" award. No, God is clear about what you and I are to do.

So, we must once again search our hearts. Instead of rating our husbands, let's check our own score in the Wife Department. How do you fare when it comes to following God's plan for a wife? Are there any pitfalls in your marriage that may be directly attributed to neglecting to do things God's way? Is there any tension caused by a failure to adhere to God's recipe for a happy marriage, a recipe made up of four basic ingredients: *help, submit, respect,* and *love?*

To help us apply God's teaching, I've put these four biblical elements into an easy-to-remember formula using the word W-I-F-E.

Warm up his life with your love

Improve his life as a helper

Follow his leadership with a willing heart

Esteem him highly with utmost respect

But What If...?

I have to stop right here and address two situations many wives (perhaps you, dear one?) find themselves in. I can almost hear you wondering...

"But what if I'm married to a man who is not a Christian?" Very briefly, God's Word and your roles still stand in such a marriage. Your job from God is not to change your husband or to save him. Both of these results occur by a divine, supernatural work that only God can accomplish in a husband's heart. Your assignment from God is to love, follow, assist, and minister to your non-Christian husband while living in a Christlike manner before his eyes. Also, you cannot expect a husband who is not a Christian to act like a man who is. Remember, too, that God can help you do anything...including love an unbeliever.

"But what if I'm married to a 'passive' Christian?" This is a husband who is a Christian, but who will not provide leadership. What-

> *Your assignment from God is not to change your husband, but to love, follow, assist, and minister to him.*

ever you ask, the answer you receive is "It's up to you," "Whatever you want," or "It doesn't matter to me." Again, your roles still stand in such a marriage—you are to help, follow, respect, and love your mate. You will definitely want to learn better ways of asking for direction and for discussing the issues in your marriage and family. You will also want to guard your heart against frustration and bitterness and guard your mouth against criticism, put-downs, and blow-ups. Two wrongs do not make a right. Your mate's failure to lead does not give you the right to sin.[3]

I regret that space is so limited in this book to discuss this vital area of marriage. Indeed, entire books have been written on living out the roles of a wife in a variety of marriage situations. But help for any Christian woman's marriage comes first from these few simple basics. So check again: As a wife, how are you measuring up in the four key areas (help, follow, respect, and love)? A wife after God's own heart desires to follow God's perfect plan...with all her heart.

Back to the Basics

If you're like me, no matter how long you've been married or how wonderful your husband is, you've probably pinpointed a weak area or two on your side of your marriage. After all, no wife is perfect: There is always room for improvement, and there are always items to be placed on the "Needs Improvement" list. I know in my life the four key areas seem to go in cycles. Just when I get one under control, a red flag starts waving in another. And then I have to stop, pray, revisit God's blueprint, and refresh my commitment to follow His plan for my part of my marriage. Back to the basics I go!

And here's something else I've discovered. As I am writing this chapter, Jim and I have been married 38 years. I've found that, like other areas of my life, our marriage has its "seasons." For instance, we experienced the season of child-raising and its wear-and-tear demands on us as a couple. Sometimes I didn't approve of Jim's way of disciplining our children. At other times I thought he should spend more time with them. And then we had to agree on how, when, and where we would take vacations (not to mention how we would pay for them!). At each season and step along the way—through the preschool years, the grade school, junior high, and high school years—evaluations and adjustments had to be made. You see, even though I was going through these stages and phases as a *mother,* I was also going through them as a *wife.* And Jim and I, as a couple, had to go through them together. We had to work as a team in order to meet the challenges and make it through.

Then we moved into our girls' college years—years when our daughters came and went. One day it was just the two of us...and the next day they would show up with a gang of friends. These were the days, too, when young men began to show up, adding new elements to the mix...and new tests to our marriage and family. Again, Jim and I went through these days as parents, but we also had to go through them as a couple. This meant we were constantly fine-tuning, re-tuning, and re-turning to our basic roles of leading and following. (This is also why the next chapter on communication is so important—it takes a great deal of communicating to work as a team!)

In God's timing, we next entered the period of being the parents of newlyweds—a whole new remarkable-but-different season as we had to figure out our new roles in our daughters' lives and welcome two wonderful sons-in-law into our family. Again the adjustments had to be made... together.

Then came Jim's transition from being a full-time professor at a theological seminary to being a full-time, stay-at-home writer. How does a wife go from 35 years of getting her husband off to work to suddenly working alongside him every minute of every day? (And you would not believe the number of women who have asked me to write a book on this "season"!) What *did* I do? Once again, back to the drawing board I went—God's drawing board! And, sure enough, nothing had changed. I was still to help, follow, respect, and love my husband as we entered this surprisingly joyous season of marriage.

Jim and I have endured—and enjoyed!—a few other seasons, too, such as the deaths of all our parents and the addition of grandbabies to our family mix. And I know there are more seasons (Lord willing!) awaiting us as we continue to grow in our marriage. But I also know that God's rules, God's guidelines, God's precepts for me as a wife will never change. They make up His unchanging plan for me as a wife, as well as for you as a wife.

> *Your commitment to follow God's plan makes a difference in the atmosphere in your home and improves the climate of your marriage.*

Making a Difference

So now I ask you to please stop, pray, and revisit God's blueprint. Refresh your commitment to actively follow His plan for your roles in your marriage. And remember, the goal is to work together as a team, today and every day throughout life and its seasons.

Your commitment to follow God's plan for a wife makes a tremendous difference. How? It will make a difference in the atmosphere in your home, in your communication as a couple, in your heart as love for your husband blossoms and abounds, and in the way you treat him with greater respect. It will also improve the climate of your marriage, paving the way for the two of you to dwell together in harmony. And the children? They will be the blessed inhabitants of a pleasant and peaceful home-sweet-home!

Dear fellow wife, when you and I are faithful to follow God's plan for us, the possibilities are spectacular. The Bible refers to the following possible by-His-grace changes that can occur in your husband and family as you, the wife, faithfully follow God's plan.

☞ *Sanctification of the unbeliever*—The unbelieving partner and the children of a mixed marriage (one believer and one unbeliever) are "sanctified." In other words, "one Christian in a marriage brings grace that spills over on the spouse."[4] This means your husband—and children—are privileged to participate in the protection of God and the opportunity of being in close contact with you as a believer, as a member of God's family (1 Corinthians 7:14).

☞ *Salvation of the unbeliever*—The condition described above (being a partaker of the blessings God bestows on a believing wife) can ease the path to conversion for the unbelieving spouse and children.[5] Your unsaved husband may become "saved" (by God's grace!) as he partakes of God's blessing in your life and witnesses Spirit-filled behavior (1 Corinthians 7:14,16).

🕊 *Spiritual life*—An unbelieving husband might (again, by God's great grace!) be "won over" to Christ, or a nominal, lackluster Christian mate (like the passive husband referred to in this chapter) might be stirred to spiritual growth as a result of your godly conduct (1 Peter 3:1-2).

I repeat, the possibilities are spectacular...and the blessings unending and eternal! Why would we *not* take action to become wives after God's own heart today?

"Two Are Better Than One"

I hope and pray you are beginning to taste and embrace the magnitude—and the beauty—of being a wife after God's own heart. And, oh, the blessings! I love the scripture verse at the beginning of this chapter about working as a team. Actually, there are two verses that go together:

> *Two are better than one,*
> *because they have a good reward for their labor.*
> *For if they fall, one will lift up his companion.*
> *But woe to him who is alone when he falls,*
> *for he has no one to help him up.*
> ECCLESIASTES 4:9-10

These verses paint a picture of some of the blessings of marriage. It's obvious that a "team" of two people who work together well will get more done. Also the work is done more quickly and efficiently. Plus the quality of teamwork can be superior to the efforts of one person. And in a twosome there's someone to help you through the difficult times, as well as someone to share your joys. There is no substitute for the help, compassion, companionship, care, and strength that bless a couple when they work as a team. Truly, two—you and your dear husband—are better than one!

Heart Response

If you are like most women, you capture your precious memories on camera and then place them in a photo album...and pore over them later by the hour. I know I never go anywhere without my camera in my pocket or purse. No, I don't want to miss a single once-in-a-lifetime photo opportunity!

Well, my friend, we have just been allowed to peek into God's photo album of His prize-winning couple. Indeed, they are a winning combination and stand forever as a model for us to learn from and emulate. The husband leads, loves, and works hard to provide, while the wife follows, loves, helps, and appreciates his efforts. Why not purpose to follow after God's plan with all your heart, soul, mind, and strength (and that's what it's going to take!), to become a wife after God's own heart?

Little Things That Make a Big Difference

1. Thank your husband for living out his roles.

Specifically remark on a decision your husband has made regarding the direction the two of you will take. Thank him that he works hard on his job. Instead of complaining because he gets home late or puts in extra hours or goes the extra mile at work, praise him for his diligence, his desire to do things excellently, and his efforts in providing for you and your family. Let him know, too, that you notice the many ways he helps you, "the weaker vessel," out. These are ways that your husband expresses his love for you, so thank him! And don't worry if he doesn't do these things. Just keep your eyes and ears—and your heart!—open so they catch the ways that he does express his love. Then, of course, thank him!

2. Ask your husband how you can help.

Every day ask your husband two questions: "What can I do for you today?" and "What can I do to help you make better use of your time today?" Stand by with a notepad and pen in hand, a prayer in your heart, and a willingness to help your husband in the ways he believes he can best be helped.

3. Show greater respect for your husband.

God wants you to *show* your respect for your husband. So think of one way you can do just that. Then, of course, follow through. Let your admiration shine forth for all to see, especially him! Do you look at him when he's talking? Do you refrain from interrupting? Do you ask him to do things instead of telling him? Do you practice sweet speech in your conversations? Do you need to stop putting him down when you talk to others? It wouldn't hurt to keep a list of ways to show respect as a reminder...in case you slip up. It happens!

4. Think of a way the two of you can have fun this week.

Later we'll enjoy an entire chapter on this fun aspect that really matters in a happy marriage (see Chapter 10). For now, though, your marriage was founded on friendship, and you need to nurture that friendship "love" spoken of in Titus 2:4. So be creative! Your fun time together doesn't have to cost any money—only the price of your time to think of an activity, set it up, and make it happen. Let the fun begin!

5. Pray to follow God's plan for a wife.

Consider God's four guidelines for you as a wife (see Genesis 2:18; Ephesians 5:22; Ephesians 5:33; and Titus 2:4) and pray over them. Take your time and express your heart to God. Make your commitments, purpose in your heart to pursue God's plan for you in each area, and then move ahead through your day seeking to comply with God's blueprint for a wife. To stay on your wifely toes, pray every day to be a wife after God's own heart!

6. Seek out another woman as a mentor.

Look around for a woman who is doing a good job at being a Christian wife—one who can help you become a better teammate to your husband. Phone her and ask to meet with her one time. Then go to your get-together with a list of questions in hand. No price can be put on the wisdom, guidance, and support a more spiritually mature woman can give you as you grow into God's kind of wife!

3

*L*earning to *C*ommunicate

Sweetness of the lips increases learning.
The heart of the wise teaches his mouth,
and adds learning to his lips.
PROVERBS 16:21,23

*M*ost every bride returns home from her honey-moon with stars in her eyes and dreams in her heart about the romantic road that stretches endlessly ahead of her and her beloved. I know I did. Jim's and my honeymoon was brief—only two days long—because we had to be at work on the Tuesday that followed our Memorial Day weekend wedding. *Never mind,* I thought, *we have the rest of our lives to be together!* Truly, it seemed like we were standing on the threshold of a lifetime of joy, love, excitement, and passion.

But on that day when Jim returned to work and I went to my job on the university campus, real life set in. I walked to my nine-to-five job, while Jim commuted an hour in heavy traffic to Oklahoma City to his job at the pharmacy inside a large Costco-type warehouse. Jim worked until nine o'clock at night, only to face another one-hour drive back home. When he staggered through the door that first night, dead tired, I conceded, *Well, there goes our first amorous dinner and our first love-filled night in our first-ever "home"* (albeit a one-bedroom apartment). This scene was repeated for the remainder of our first should-have-been-blissful week, until Saturday arrived ...and Jim staggered out the door at four o'clock in the morning to travel to his monthly two-day weekend U.S. Army Reserve meeting. When he arrived home in the dark Sunday night and fell into bed so he could get up the next day and begin his daily commute to work for yet another week, we both realized we had some adjustments to make.

Every couple has their bouts with reality checks and fine-tuning. And every couple has to learn how to communicate so the needed adjustments can be made more smoothly. All couples have to do the communicating and the adjusting over...and over...and over again as the issues and challenges of life change, not only daily, but also within each day.

Thank goodness God's Word gives us guidelines not only for our marriages but for our communication. The Bible tells couples like you and your husband the best way to share and receive information as you work your way through emotions, disappointments, and confusions to reach solutions to the barrage of challenges you encounter. So pay attention! The section that follows is a lifesaver...and a marriage-saver!

"Like Apples of Gold..."

In poetic language the writer of Proverbs 25:11 paints this word picture of good communication:

> *A word fitly spoken is like*
> *apples of gold in settings of silver.*

Dear wife, this kind of beauty should be the goal for all of your communication, but especially with the person most important and closest to you—your husband. So here are several of God's keys to godly speech. Your words are to be...

...*soft*. "A soft answer turns away wrath, but a harsh word stirs up anger" (Proverbs 15:1). The words we choose to use have an effect on the hearer. Harsh, loud, caustic speech leads to arguments and quarrels, while soft, gentle words bring about peace. And here's another fact: "A soft tongue can break hard bones" (Proverbs 25:15 TLB)!

...*sweet*. "Sweetness of the lips increases learning" or influence (Proverbs 16:21). Do you want to get your point across? Then realize that "pleasant words promote instruction" and understanding (16:21 NIV).

...*suitable*. "Pleasant words are like a honeycomb, sweetness to the soul and health to the bones" (Proverbs 16:24). Kind, sweet words have a medicinal effect on both body and soul.

...*scant.* "In the multitude of words sin is not lacking,
but he who restrains his lips is wise" (Proverbs
10:19). The more you talk, the more you are sure
to sin! Another Bible translation is very vivid and
down-to-earth in its language: "Don't talk so
much. You keep putting your foot in your mouth.
Be sensible and turn off the flow!"[1] As someone
put it, "Sometimes the most skillful use of the
tongue is keeping it still."[2]

...*slow.* "Be swift to hear, slow to speak, slow to wrath"
(James 1:19). In even fewer words, make it your
aim to "listen much, speak little, and not become
angry" (TLB)! Why? Because "the wrath of man
does not produce the righteousness of God" (verse
20 NKJV). No good ever comes from sinful anger.

Do you want your speech to be like apples of gold in
settings of silver? Like 14-carat gold fruit in a sterling silver
basket? Priceless? Indescribable? Admirable? Exquisite?
Desirable? Then learn to speak with godly wisdom when
you communicate with your husband. Choose words that
are soft, sweet, suitable, and, by all means, scant.

"Like a Constant Dripping"

What happens when you and I don't communicate
God's way? What results from a failure to pay attention to
God's wise guidelines for our speech? Proverbs has more
word pictures for us, detailed in these verses:

"The contentions of a wife are a continual dripping" (Proverbs 19:13).

"Better to dwell in a corner of a housetop, than in a house shared with a contentious woman" (Proverbs 21:9).

"Better to dwell in the wilderness, than with a contentious and angry woman" (Proverbs 21:19).

"A continual dripping on a very rainy day and a contentious woman are alike" (Proverbs 27:15).

I'm sure you get the picture! The message is that a crabby, cranky, nagging, quarrelsome, complaining, ill-tempered wife annoys her husband in the same way a constant drip gets on our nerves and "drives us crazy." In fact, as these proverbs report, it not only drives a husband crazy, but it can also drive him away. To escape the constant drip, drip, drip of a wife's sour, negative words, a husband will choose to live in the attic, on the porch, on the rooftop, or even in the wilds. He would rather risk the elements, do without the shelter and comfort of home, even take his chances against the threat of wild animals than stay one more second in the presence of a belligerent wife.

> *Make it your goal to employ the sweet speech that marks you as a wife after God's own heart.*

So I urge you to evaluate your speech patterns. Ask God to reveal if you are falling into the "contentious" category...or if you are articulating the sweet speech that marks you as a wife after God's own heart. Are you majoring on yourself or are you majoring on your husband—on helping, following, respecting, and loving him? Are you a listener or a whimperer? Do your words minister a calming influence or do they resemble a raging torrent of destruction?

Performing Radical Surgery

If you don't like your evaluation of your communication tactics and topics or the results of such tactics and topics (and, believe me, every wife falters and fails in this area!), then something has got to change. Radical surgery must be performed on your heart and your tongue. I'm sure you desire to utter words that are fitting of a wife after God's own heart—words that are pleasing to the Lord and that portray you as a wise and sympathetic wife. I'm sure you wish for your speech to minister to your husband and edify your relationship with him.

So I'm suggesting that, in order to turn the corner on your communication, you must...

Take it to the Lord in prayer—Pour out your struggles, disappointments, complaints, bitterness, fears, and failures to God. That's what dear Hannah did. Hannah was a woman and wife after God's own heart. There's no doubt that she had an extremely difficult marriage and family situation. To begin her list of woes, she was married to a man who had two wives. And to top that off, "Hannah had no children" (1 Samuel 1:2). The other wife, however, did. But Hannah's heartaches didn't stop there. Adding insult to injury, the other wife "provoked her severely, to make her miserable, because the LORD had closed her womb" (verse 6).

What was Hannah's solution? As we discuss the answer, note this too—Hannah is one of the few women in the Bible about whom nothing negative is reported. To our knowledge, gained by what is—and isn't—reported in the Bible, Hannah didn't lash out at her husband or at his other wife. What did she do instead? When Hannah "was in bitterness of soul...[she] prayed to the LORD" (verse 10). In His presence she wept in anguish and silently prayed in her heart before the Lord, pleading with Him and vowing to Him about the issues in her miserable home life (verses 10-13).

Do you perhaps have an unbearable, seemingly impossible situation at home? What under your roof tries and tests your soul? Name it—and then take it to the Lord in prayer. In His presence you may express all that you feel and fear. You can divulge your personal bitterness of soul. Precious reader, thank God that you and I "do not have a High Priest who cannot sympathize with our weaknesses, but was in all points tempted as we are, yet without sin. Let us therefore come boldly to the throne of grace, that we may obtain mercy and find grace to help in time of need"

(Hebrews 4:15-16). Let us *boldly* take our problems to the Lord in prayer.

Make a decision to "cut it out"—While you are pouring out your heart to God admitting your faults in the Communications Department, confess your failures in the Sweet Speech Department. Then ask God to help you do "radical surgery" on your speech. Seek His help in cutting out and eliminating the practices, words, decibel levels, and emotions that go against His communication principles, that fail to honor Him, and that fail to accomplish His will for your mouth.

This principle of drastic action comes from a lesson taught by Jesus when He told offenders of God's law how to deal with the eye or hand that sins. He said of the eye to "pluck it out," and of the hand to "cut it off" (Matthew 5:29-30). As you can see, Jesus called for radical surgery!

Beloved, you and I, as women after God's own heart who desire to be wives after God's own heart, must treat our sinful speech patterns in a drastic way. They are wrong, unproductive, even counterproductive. They do not accomplish the will or purposes of God (James 1:20). Therefore, we must be done with such speech. In short, we must "cut it out"!

So please, partner with God. Ask for His help in curbing wild, rampant, destructive, and ungodly speech. Yet another proverb tells us, "There is one who speaks like the piercings of a sword, but the tongue of the wise promotes health" (Proverbs 12:18). Your communication with your husband (or anyone!) will improve a thousand percent when you cease wielding the sword of rash, venomous words.

If you want to be wise, then remember that "in the multitude of words sin is not lacking, but he who restrains his lips is wise" (Proverbs 10:19). A sure way to be wise—and to cut it out—is to restrain your lips. Just say nothing. Try it for a day. It will be difficult, but it will be the best day of your life...and of your husband's, too! It will be a day marked by wisdom.

> *Wise, godly speech and increased persuasiveness is all about how you say what you say.*

And it will be a day of glorious victory, peace, and self-control you'll want to mark on your calendar. It will be a day lived as a wife after God's own heart.

Proceeding Ahead

In a previous chapter we learned that companionship is one of the benefits and blessings of marriage. As Solomon observed, "Two are better than one." Of course you and I as wives should be able to share our concerns with our husbands. But wise, godly speech like "apples of gold in settings of silver" and increased persuasiveness is all about *how* we say what we say. It's when we fail in these laws of sweet speech that we have to...

- 🌷 come to a halt (say nothing),

- 🌷 take a break (from our old and unsuccessful ways of communicating),

    🐝   take a step backward (pray and search our hearts),

    🐝   regroup (make a decision to do it God's way), and then

    🐝   proceed ahead.

That's what I had to do, over...and over...and over again. I remember it all too well. At the time when our daughters were preschoolers, my Jim had four (yes, four!) jobs. Jim had resigned from his pharmaceutical sales job to answer his "call" to ministry and go back to school for theological training. And, bless his heart, this dear man did not want me to go to work with two little ones in the home. This was a time when not only did I wish Jim could spend more time with our girls, but I wished he could spend more time with *me!*

At first I handled our new situation in the wrong way. I whined. When that didn't work, I cried. When that didn't work, I screamed. When that didn't work, I stomped and sulked, making good use of "the cold shoulder." What a brat I was!

God's Better Way

But then I began growing in my knowledge of the Bible. Soon I understood more about Jim's roles as a Christian husband (one role was to *provide* for his family). I also understood more about my roles as a Christian wife (one being to *help* Jim). And I also discovered God's good-better-and-best methods of communication—the ones we are discussing in this chapter. I knew in my Spirit-convicted heart that something had to give. Something had to change. So, my friend, here is what I did in my efforts to learn to communicate God's way. I began...

...learning to pray. At the first hint of frustration or self-pity, I prayed.

...learning to say nothing. Whenever my emotions approached the danger point, I again prayed, and then did whatever was required to stop the flow by saying nothing.

...learning to wait. I knew Jim was tired and almost stretched to the limit (and so was I!). By God's grace, I learned to wait for the right time to communicate. For us that became once a week during our 89-cent Coke date at the fast-food restaurant across the street while an angelic neighbor watched Katherine and Courtney.

...learning to make a list. While I waited, I faithfully and carefully—and prayerfully—wrote down everything I felt Jim and I needed to talk through. This list included issues like methods of disciplining our daughters, decisions that needed to be made, and financial concerns. (The chapter on finances is coming up soon!)

...learning to make an appointment. If our Coke date wasn't going to work out, I would approach Jim and schedule another time for us to talk about pressing matters. By doing this, Jim could pick the time that was best and most convenient for him. From that moment on, we both anticipated the exact time for our talk.

...learning to write it out. Many times I would, with much prayer, write out the exact words I wanted to say—how I wanted to "present my case" and any options or solutions I had thought of. I learned this from Proverbs 15:28—"The heart of the righteous *studies* how to answer, but the mouth of the wicked pours forth evil."

...learning "to take the blame." This is my own phrase for communicating about serious issues with "a meek and quiet spirit" (1 Peter 3:4 KJV). My principle drawn from these guiding words for women was (and still is), "Meekness takes the blame." Let me explain. With this motto in mind, I would say to my husband, "I'm having a problem understanding this...or seeing how this can work...or accepting this change. Can you help me out...or help me with my thinking?" Without this motto in mind, my mouth would automatically blurt out something hostile and accusing like, "Why do you always..." or "Your idea is stupid" or "How come you don't..." Did you note the difference? You and I can begin our sentences with "I" or with "you." The choice is ours.

And I've found that when I begin with "I" (as in "*I'm* having a problem understanding this" instead of "Your idea is stupid"), our communication as a couple goes much more smoothly.

Now, how's that for "learning" to communicate? Needless to say, these seven disciplines (and there are more) put me—and my marriage—on the path to improved communication and increased blessings. And they can do the same for you!

Heart Response

I love music, orchestras, and concerts. Perhaps that's because I played the violin in my junior high school orchestra. I like to think that I did my part and made a positive contribution to the group and those in our audiences.

But what do you think would have happened if, on Day One of my violin undertaking, I grabbed my new school-issued violin, ran onto the concert stage, plopped down in a chair, and began playing with the other members of the group? What a racket you would have heard! What squeaks, screeches, squawks, and scratches you would have been forced to endure!

But, no. Both you and I know what it requires to play in harmony in any setting, whether in an orchestra, in a choir, in a drama troupe, on a sports team...or in a marriage. It requires learning the proper techniques. And it demands time as you practice, practice, practice!

If I could say one thing to you after reading through this important chapter on this oh-so-vital skill of communicating with your husband, I would say this: Don't just run in to talk to your husband, plop down, grab at anything your sometimes-empty brain finds handy, and blurt out thoughtless or insensitive words. Instead take the time to prepare your heart and your words. Pray about timing, tone, and topics. Ask God for help with godly discipline over the thoughts of your heart and the words of your mouth (see Psalm 19:14). Make it your aim to convey information, to bless your precious husband, and to create harmony. Seek to do an excellent job of verbalizing your heart to your husband in a godly way and with godly wisdom. By all means, make an effort and take the time to learn—and apply—God's rules for communication. You'll be glad you did. And I guarantee your husband will, too!

Little Things That Make a Big Difference

1. Follow God's guidelines for good communication.

Are your words soft, sweet, suitable, scant, and slow? Begin reminding yourself each day to "put away" speech patterns that don't match up to God's standards and to put these five elements of wholesome communication in their place instead. Ask God to guide you when you are communicating with your husband.

2. Identify any speech patterns that must go.

Read Jesus' words about "radical surgery" in Matthew 5:29-30. As you consider your speech, what must go—at any cost!—and when? (And remember, delayed obedience is disobedience.) By making a decision to "cut it out," praying faithfully, sprinkling a few well-placed sticky-note reminders around the house, and, of course, by the mighty grace of God, you can give it up.

I still remember going through such an exercise (and exorcise-ing!) when I became convicted about screaming at my two little preschoolers. I knew it was wrong and destructive. And yet I did it...until I reached the radical surgery stage. Sure, there were slip-ups. And sure, change took a l-o-n-g time! But progress was made day-by-day, decision-by-decision, word-by-word. God enabled me to grow and to change in a way that bettered our home life and blessed my family. Again, what must go—at any cost!—and when?

3. Make it a goal to encourage your husband.

Have you ever been wounded by the "wieldings" of someone else's sharp tongue (see Proverbs 12:18)? And worse yet, have you ever done damage to another person in the same way, with your words (like I did when I screamed at my little girls)? Your goal as a wife after God's own heart is to help, heal, and minister to your husband with your words— not to slash and slice him to pieces. Your rash words can resemble the thrusts of a sword or they can disperse refreshment that promotes health, edifies, encourages, and delivers grace to your husband (Ephesians 4:29).

Words

A careless word may kindle strife.
A cruel word may wreck a life.
A brutal word may smite and kill.
A gracious word may smooth the way.
A joyous word may light the day.
A timely word may lessen stress.
A loving word may heal and bless.

4. Be quick to say you're sorry.

The sooner you can say you are sorry for temper, for negative responses, for hurtful words, or for sinful attitudes, the better! This is the quickest and best way to defuse a situation that could get worse or clear up any disturbance in your relationship with your husband so the two of you can go on with a God-pleasing life.

I've found out a few things about this "little thing." One is that whenever there is a disagreement or argument between Jim and me, everything else gets put on hold until we get things settled. No progress is made...nor is there any energy to make any progress! So we've both learned to be quick to say we're sorry. I've also learned that if I am faithfully and regularly acknowledging my sin to God, it's much easier to apologize to my husband because I'm already in the habit of saying "I'm sorry" to God.

5. "Say what you mean, but don't say it meanly!"

I like this advice from a book I purchased in an airport.[4] Enough said!

6. Seek to please God with your words.

King David of the Old Testament prayed, "Let the words of my mouth...be acceptable in Your sight, O Lord" (Psalm 19:14)! God is the first person you must please with your words. And that is the desire of every woman after God's own heart.

4

Enjoying Intimacy

> *Therefore a man shall leave his father*
> *and mother and be joined to his wife,*
> *and they shall become one flesh.*
> GENESIS 2:24

*N*ow that you are growing in the Lord, working as a team with your husband, and on the road to better communication, we finally reach the hot topic of intimacy in marriage. And believe me, you and I better be strong in the Lord, committed to our marriage, and able to communicate, because success in the Sex and Affection Department will require all three!

Created for Intimacy

I know we've already looked at the story of God's creation of mankind, but let's revisit it. That's when God created the first-ever couple, Adam and Eve. That's also when everything was perfect. All was well. In the beginning,

Adam and Eve enjoyed *perfect* intimacy because sin had not yet entered God's perfect creation.

What did the perfect marriage look like? What made up that flawless union? First of all, the environment was perfect (Genesis 1:31). It was the Garden of Eden. Also both partners—the man and the woman—were perfect. God Himself formed the man from the dust of the ground, breathing into him the breath of life (Genesis 2:7). Then God brought forth a companion, a mate, a helper, a wife, for the man from his own rib. The woman was created "from man" and "for the man" (1 Corinthians 11:8-9).

What bliss! When Adam first saw Eve, he exclaimed, "This is now bone of my bones and flesh of my flesh; she shall be called Woman, because she was taken out of Man" (Genesis 2:23). In the delightful, everyday language of another translation, Adam is reported as excitedly shouting, "This is it!...She is part of my own bone and flesh!"[1] Imagine his joy!

In the perfect environment, this perfect couple enjoyed a perfect existence...and perfect intimacy. "They found their complete gratification in the joy of their one union and their service to God."[2] As the Bible reports it, "They were both naked, the man and his wife, and were not ashamed" (Genesis 2:25).

In the Bible's account of the creation of the first marriage, God's Word lays down a principle for all married couples: "Therefore a man shall leave his father and mother and be joined to his wife, and they shall become one flesh" (verse 24). In other words, the man would "cleave" or "glue himself to" his wife.[3] The couple would begin a new and separate unit founded on intimacy.

But...What Happened?

But then something happened to the perfect place, the perfect people, their perfect marriage, and their perfect relationship with God. In a word, sin happened. The serpent tempted Eve...who listened to him instead of God (Genesis 3:1-6), Eve tempted Adam...who listened to her instead of God (Genesis 3:6)...and all was no longer perfect.

And the results? They are innumerable, my friend. And their ramifications continue around the globe to this day. But to list a few,

- sin entered God's perfect environment,

- the blissful couple who was naked and not ashamed (Genesis 2:25) was suddenly embarrassed as "they knew that they were naked" (Genesis 3:7),

- clothes were introduced for the first time as "they sewed fig leaves together and made themselves coverings" (verse 7),

- both the man and his wife were severely chastened by God (verses 16-19), and

- Adam and Eve lost their home as God drove them out and sent them away from the Garden of Eden (verses 23-24).

Beloved, there has never been such a disruption as this. And the entrance of sin spelled disruption for Adam and Eve's marital intimacy...as well as for yours and mine. Intimacy has been a struggle for all couples since the day Adam and Eve chose to listen to others instead of to God and God alone.

Rekindling Intimacy

Here's where the truth of an earlier statement comes to our rescue. I mentioned at the beginning of this chapter that the Bible contains God's forever-principles on every topic, including marriage. In His Word we learn how to rekindle, rebuild, and rediscover intimacy. From God we can learn how to overcome the sin and tension that is now a factor in every human relationship—even that between a married couple—as a result of "the Fall."

What exactly does God say a wife can do to pursue and enjoy intimacy with her husband? My answer comes from the marriage ceremony I heard performed many times at my former church by the pastor to our singles' ministry as he shared passages regarding marriage from the Scriptures with each eager bride and groom. Even without notes, I can still remember them. And the best thing is, they come from the Bible, which means they work. Hear now these why's and how's regarding sexual intimacy in marriage.

> *Proclaimed*—God proclaimed that you and your husband are to leave your parents and be joined together as "one flesh" (Genesis 2:24-25). God intends the

two of you to come together in marriage and sexual intimacy and become a new whole, complete in each other.

Procreation—God desires that the oneness created between a husband and wife in sexual intimacy result in another generation of offspring who will continue to multiply and fill the earth (Genesis 1:27-28).

Pleasure—Sexual intimacy was also designed by God to provide pleasure for both partners (Proverbs 5:15-19). This pleasure thrives as each spouse chooses to serve the other and determines not to deprive one another (1 Corinthians 7:5).

Purity—Sex within marriage is pure (Hebrews 13:4) and provides power against sexual temptation, contributing positively to the purity of both husband and wife (1 Corinthians 7:2).

Partnership—Each marriage partner has a God-given assignment to satisfy the other's physical needs and to see that his or her own needs are satisfied (1 Corinthians 7:3-4).

Protective—Sex in marriage is a safeguard against lust, temptation, and Satan's alluring, worldly tactics (1 Corinthians 7:5).

Dear reading wife, God has spoken! This is His perfect plan for sexual intimacy between you and your husband. Now, our role as wives after His own heart is to think about and perceive sex in the way He does and to fulfill His Word and His plan with our actions.

Giving Your All

As you can see, sexual pleasure in marriage is God's will, God's plan, and God's gift to both partners. Therefore you must now determine to give intimacy your all. It won't

> *Your greatest progress and victory in intimacy will be made as you choose to view, perceive, and think about sex as God does.*

be easy because what was natural and perfect at creation now requires effort. However, blessings abound as you follow after God's own heart, look to Him for help, and make the effort. What follows are a few of my personal do's and don'ts for enjoying intimacy. They have been gained from God's Word, from "giving my all," and from applying them through the

many seasons of my marriage to Jim. As you'll quickly see, three out of the four are mental assignments. Our greatest progress and victory will be made as we choose to view, perceive, and think about sex as God does. (Remember, that's where things turned bad for Adam and Eve—they failed to listen to God and listened to others instead.)

    ✧   *Do* battle against shyness and embarrassment when it comes to sex with your husband. Instead of thinking about your *self* (about what your body looks like or doesn't look like, about how you wish it looked or how you think it should look), think instead about God's perfect plan—"They were both naked...and were not ashamed" and the two became "one flesh" (Genesis 2:24-25). Think also about your husband and the pleasure your body brings to his eye (see Proverbs 5:19). After all, yours is the only body he is supposed to look at! So don't withhold it. Pray...and dive in! Give your all! Give yourself, your love, and your body to your husband in this God-ordained, God-sanctioned way.

🏵 *Do* remember that "marriage is honorable among all, and the bed undefiled" (Hebrews 13:4). In other words, sex in marriage is pure. Sex is not dirty and sex is not immoral when enjoyed with your husband. Again, pray! Ask God to dispel any thoughts that oppose His teachings regarding the right, privilege, and enjoyment He intended sex to bring to both you and your husband.

🏵 *Do* give yourself permission to delight in giving and receiving sexual pleasure during lovemaking. Enjoying intimacy is not only okay—it's God's will. Sex—and sexual pleasure—is God's perfect plan for both husband and wife. The husband in Proverbs 5:15-19 was saturated, satiated, satisfied, literally intoxicated and drunk with the sexual refreshment and affection received from his wife. And clearly, Isaac and Rebekah were enjoying some level of the excitement of sexual love as a couple when the pagan King Abimelech "looked through a window, and saw, and there was Isaac, showing endearment to Rebekah his wife. Then Abimelech called Isaac and said, 'Quite obviously she is your wife'" (Genesis 26:8-9). In other words, the king witnessed caresses that indicated marital intimacy.

☞ *Do not* withhold sex from your husband. As the Bible puts it, "Let the husband render [fulfill] to his wife the affection due her, and likewise also the wife to her husband. The wife does not have authority [or full rights] over her own body, but the husband does. And likewise the husband does not have authority [or full rights] over his own body, but the wife does. Do not deprive one another except with consent for a time, that you may give yourselves to fasting and prayer; and come together again so that Satan does not tempt you because of your lack of self-control" (1 Corinthians 7:3-5). In plain language, both husband and wife are to fulfill their marital duty to meet their spouse's normal and natural sexual needs. And marriage partners are commanded not to withhold sexually from their mate unless it is...

...by agreement,
...for a time,

...for a purpose, and

...with a prompt reunion planned.

Turning a Corner

By now I trust you are sensing from the Scriptures how highly God regards sexual intimacy in marriage and how important He intended it to be. And I pray that the verses shared have impacted your life, your heart, and your marriage. As a married woman, you are to give your all when it comes to the sexual side of your marriage. And you are to give it freely, unashamedly, joyfully, heartily, regularly, purposing not to withhold this most precious gift—and right!—from your husband.

Do you need a change of heart and attitude? If yes, how can you begin to turn a corner? How can you alter your thinking and your attitude, enhance your sex life, and improve your marriage? I'll have a good number of "little things" for you at the end of this chapter. But for now, do these two "big things."

The first, of course, is pray. Talk over this vital, foundational area of your marriage with God. He has

> *When it comes to the sexual side of your marriage, you are to give your all...freely, unashamedly joyfully, heartily, regularly.*

revealed His plan, and you and I as wives must thank Him for it. If it comes from the heart and mind of God, then it is good, perfect, and acceptable. In prayer agree with God that sex with your husband is okay, that it has His stamp

of approval, that it is one of your husband's rights and priv-
ileges in marriage, and that it is according to God's will.
And while you are praying, confess your inhibitions as self-
ishness to God. With all other men you are to be cool and
reserved physically, but not with your husband. End your
prayer time by purposing to believe what the Bible says—
to cling to it, to remember it, and to follow it. You and I, as
wives after God's own heart, are *not* going to listen to the
world. No, we are going to listen to God.

And here's the second "big thing"—Talk to your husband about your sex life. Pray about what you will say. Pray
about how you will say it (remember God's rules for good
communication!). Pray about the best time to say it. And
pray for your husband's receptivity. Your goal is to communicate to your precious mate that you want to do a
better job of being his sexual partner, that you want to
make an effort to improve. (And remember, God will help
you find the words.) If your husband is a Christian, ask
him to pray for you and with you, to encourage you, to talk
openly with you. And if he is not a Christian, go ahead and
ask him to encourage you and talk openly with you.

Trusting God

Dear wife, only God knows how...and in how many
ways...He will choose to bless you for your whole-hearted
obedience in this crucial, foundational component of your
marriage. You will have to trust Him for that. But you *will*
be blessed. Count on it! As you turn a corner and move out
in response to God and to His Word, you will be trusting

Him. For many women (perhaps you?) this is a giant step of faith. But God loves—and requires—obedience in His children. I repeat, *you will be blessed!* Don't you think one blessing to your heart will be knowing your husband is blessed? You and your husband are "heirs together of the grace of life" (1 Peter 3:7). The two of you "are partners in receiving God's blessings" (TLB). This partnership has little to do with Christianity, but much to do with marriage, for marriage is "the best relationship earthly life has to offer."[4]

Heart Response

How I wish I could see you and talk to you in person. How I would love to know exactly where you need encouragement. But I can't, so I'll just have to speak my heart to you based on the mail I receive and on the concerns of the many women I have talked with. And why were they contacting me? The three most recent women were motivated to seek help and advice because they were fortunate enough to have husbands who spoke up honestly and shared their bouts with sexual temptation, suffering, irritableness, and sexual frustration. The bottom line in each case was the husband's desire for sexual intimacy more often. And as I listened and empathized, prayed and searched for words to comfort, exhort, and encourage these dear sisters-in-Christ, it was the scriptures we have shared together in this chapter that came to my mind and out of my mouth.

I know there are different and even difficult scenarios in each woman's unique marital situation. I recognize that there are problems...and there are problem-husbands. And I thank God there are pastors, counselors, and wise older women to help us with the application of God's principles in our individual circumstances. Perhaps you are a wife who needs to share your situation with one of these wise people. If so, I encourage you to do so. Also there are many books written that address a variety of conditions. I recommend that you read these books. But in the meantime—and always—you have God's Word to guide you. When in doubt, check it out! "What does God have to say about sexual intimacy, and how can I make giant strides in applying His guidelines to my marriage?" You will be helped and blessed each and every time you implement His truth and follow His instructions! As I said before, they work!

Little Things That Make a Big Difference

1. Take your calendar in hand and schedule sex!

How does that sound to you? Cold? Sterile? Unemotional? Lacking in romance? But talking openly with your husband and planning ahead as a couple can revolutionize your sex life. Intimacy doesn't just happen, you know. So to ensure that it does for you and your hubby, schedule it. Talking with your husband with calendar in hand also gives him an opportunity to express the frequency he'd like to see in the Intimacy Department of your marriage. After all, according to the records kept by one marriage counselor, when asked to create their Top-Five List of "most basic needs," time and time again husbands expressed that "#1" was "sexual fulfillment."[5] And note this too—When wives were asked for the same information, sex did not appear at all on the Top-Five List!

2. Talk about sex with your husband.

We just spent one chapter on communication, and here is a primary place to put the principles to work for you...and start talking! If the two of you can communicate joyfully, seriously, lovingly, tenderly, and specifically, then the two of you can steadily move toward greater enjoyment of intimacy.

After all, you'll want to be enjoying sex for a l-o-n-g time! Two counselors reported these encouraging findings: "In our national survey on long-term marriage, we discovered that sexual satisfaction actually goes up, not down, for those married thirty-plus years."[6]

3. Take time to prepare for sex.

Just like a gourmet meal takes time in preparation, so do your intimate times together. Think about it...enjoying a full-blown meal requires creating a menu, searching for the right recipes, making a list of ingredients, taking a trip to the store to gather the necessary items, putting out the money for the goods, spending time cooking in the kitchen, time setting the table, time making the atmosphere just so, and then time to serve, time to partake, and time to savor. The same applies to your times of lovemaking with your husband. You need to schedule and allow time...to think, to pray, to prepare, to run to the store to purchase something special, to set the scene and the mood, to enjoy, to linger. Wow, what a "feast" that will be! Lucky husband! Lucky you!

4. Try to go to bed at the same time.

Is this "little thing" ever important in the Good Sex Department! Sure, there may be times and careers that require that the husband go to bed before his wife, but in many marriages this is not the case. The wife simply chooses to stay up later than her husband. So here's a question for you: How can you cuddle, be available sexually, and not to mention get a good night's sleep yourself if you and your husband don't go to bed together?

5. Tackle the excuse of "I'm too tired!"

And what woman isn't? (I'm chuckling as I write about tiredness!) But you're a smart woman. You know how to run a home, raise children, perhaps homeschool your children, or excel on your job. So you also know how to figure out what has to be cut back or cut out of your life so that you're not too tired for this most-important part of your life—your sex life. Your assignment is to find the culprits that are robbing you of sleeptime and change them so you are not too tired to enjoy sex with your husband, not to mention improving your health and well-being! (P.S. It wouldn't hurt to have your sweetie's input on your analysis.)

6. Take care of yourself.

There are many little ways you can make yourself more attractive for your husband. Good grooming costs only a few minutes. So why not clean up, fix up, dress up, makeup...a little? Also a little exercise goes a long way! A 20-minute walk, five days a week, will cause you to tone your body and lose 12 pounds in a year without ever changing what you eat. Plus losing a little weight never hurts in the Lovemaking Department. Every woman puts on a few pounds while fulfilling her role as chief cook, while bearing children, and while centering her life at home. If this is your case, losing those pounds will give you energy *and* breathe fresh life into your sex life.

7. Take a short trip together.

A good, old-fashioned getaway can also refresh your marriage and buy you time for prolonged intimacy, conversations, dreaming, planning, and plain ol' fun! Children are a blessing, but once they begin arriving, time alone together must be planned. With planning, prayer, and preparation, you can take a nice 24-hour getaway for a very small amount of money.

5

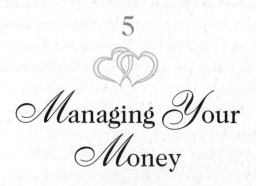

Managing Your Money

Who can find a virtuous wife?
For her worth is far above rubies.
The heart of her husband safely trusts her;
so he will have no lack of gain.
PROVERBS 31:10-11

*M*y husband, Jim, recently gave me a startling statistic that revealed the importance of wise money management in marriage. He said he had read that almost 90 percent of all marital arguments can be traced back to the issue of money.

And not too long after Jim shared this information with me, I viewed a television commercial that humorously backed it up. The scene was the delivery room in a hospital where a woman was in the throes of giving birth. As the soon-to-be-mother's labor progressed, more procedures and medications were being provided to assist the birth.

The nervous husband stood by, wringing his hands. To the doctor he said words equivalent to, "Can I assist you? Do you really need so many nurses?" To the anesthesiologist he questioned, "Are you sure she requires an epidural?" To his wife he said, "Honey, it's been 36 hours. Can't you hurry this up?"

Then the narrated pitch came, and I discovered that the ad was for medical insurance...and the issue was money. And there you have it—a glimpse at the way money matters can eat its dismal way into every phase of a married couple's life, including the joy of welcoming a baby into their happy union!

Money Matters to God

As we step into this all-important chapter, I want to explain that I am moving us through the issues and aspects of a married couple's life in a particular order. First, as a wife after God's own heart, we noted that every part and parcel of your life begins with a strong relationship and commitment to God. Then we addressed knowing and living out the roles that God's Word lays down for us as wives so that we contribute our part to the husband–wife team. I placed communication next because everything in a couple's life must be discussed so decisions can be made and principles established. Then came intimacy as a key to a happy marriage.

And now I believe we must address finances. Why? Because before you have a roof over your head and before children are added to your family unit, money matters must be dealt with. Even before the wedding, money is a heavy concern as a couple wrestles through questions such as "Can we make it financially?" and "How will we pay for the wedding?"

Not only is money important to an engaged couple, a married couple, and a full-blown family (right up to and through retirement and the sunset years), but it matters to God. Let's hear from Him through His Word about this minute-by-minute concern in every marriage.

Money is to be earned. And that requires hard work. Remember the role of the husband as established by Genesis 3:17-19? God told Adam that he would have to eat and provide "in toil" and "in the sweat of [his] face." I realize that in many marriages the wife also contributes to the family income. But my point here is that God intends that income be earned by intense, earnest work and effort, rather than by being stolen or gained by lying, cheating, begging, or fraud.

> *"Wealth gained by dishonesty will be diminished, but he who gathers by labor will increase."*

Note the work ethic in these proverbs. Regarding money gained in sinful ways, Proverbs 10:2 states, "Treasures of wickedness profit nothing." Regarding laziness, begging, and mooching, Proverbs 10:4 teaches, "He who has a slack hand becomes poor, but the hand of the diligent makes rich." Putting these principles together, Proverbs 13:11 reports,

"Wealth gained by dishonesty will be diminished, but he who gathers by labor will increase." And Proverbs 28:19 adds, "He who tills his land will have plenty of bread, but he who follows frivolity will have poverty enough!"

Money is to be given. After money is earned, this next principle from God must be put into immediate application. Your money comes from God (Deuteronomy 8:18) and is to be used for Him, His purposes, and His people. Therefore, Christians are to give of their money regularly and purposefully, sacrificially, generously, and cheerfully.[1] Certainly others benefit from your giving as burdens are eased and ministries are funded. So follow in the faithful footsteps of the wise home-manager in Proverbs 31: "She extends her hand to the poor, yes, she reaches out her hands to the needy" (verse 20).

And here's an added bonus! Not only do others benefit, but you do, too. As our Lord Jesus taught, instead of laying up "treasures on earth," you are to "lay up for yourselves treasures in heaven...for where your treasure is, there your heart will be also" (Matthew 6:19-21). A woman—and a wife—after God's own heart tends to her heart by tending to her giving.

Money is to be managed and saved. Next comes the stewardship of God's money. Character is needed and bred as you learn thrift, diligence, carefulness, self-control, the virtue of waiting, and the skills of saving, stretching, record-keeping, and wise decision-making. By keen oversight of the finances, yours can be a house (and marriage!)

of peace and plenty. As Proverbs promises, "Through wisdom a house is built, and by understanding it is established; by knowledge the rooms are filled with all precious and pleasant riches" (Proverbs 24:3-4). Your family unit, your character, and your enterprises will be blessed as you respond to God's assignment to you as a wife and home-manager to studiously and painstakingly manage and save money for the good of your loved ones.

Money is not to be desired. As Christians we are to beware of greed and the love of money. We are to "be rich in good works, ready to give, willing to share" (1 Timothy 6:18). As a few more proverbs put it, "Better is a little with righteousness, than vast revenues without justice" and "better is a little with the fear of the LORD, than great treasure with trouble" (Proverbs 16:8 and 15:16). As the apostle Paul exhorted, rather than greediness, desiring to be rich, and loving and chasing after money, we are to "flee these things and pursue righteousness, godliness, faith, love, patience, gentleness" (1 Timothy 6:11). Dear one, your riches will one day be gone (verse 7). Therefore realize that "godliness with contentment is great gain" (verse 6).

Money Matters in Marriage

Knowing a little more of what God says about money, and knowing that it is His money and that we as wives are, in our own sphere and in our own way, stewards of His money, it is time to make some decisions. Will we or won't we follow God's perfect plan? Will we or won't we heed His desires and instruction? Exactly what will we do with the money He entrusts to us for faithful management? And exactly what is it that we desire to do with money?

I've written extensively on the money management of the woman portrayed as God's ideal wife in Proverbs 31:10-31.[2] And I can still remember the complete makeover of my heart, my head, my home, and my marriage as I witnessed this incredible woman's making and management of finances for her dear family. Threaded throughout the 22 verses that make up her portrait is the theme of money and money management. Her character qualities shine as she "girds" herself physically to do the work (verse 17), uses her mind to budget and increase the family funds, and creates goods to barter and sell to further benefit her beloved family. As a result, God was honored (verse 30), the poor were served (verse 20), her husband was elevated (verse 23), and she was known by all as "a virtuous wife" (verse 10). "*Her* worth" to her husband, children, and community was "far above rubies" (verse 10).

That's what I want for you (and me), my friend! I want you to represent the Lord and His will well (Titus 2:5). And I want you to be a blessing, first and foremost to your dear sweet husband. I want you to grow in character, be content with what you have, support your husband's efforts, and be a diligent homemaker and financial warrior as you "build your home" (see Proverbs 14:1). I want you to be a woman filled with every good virtue and God's fruit of the Spirit (Galatians 5:22-23). And your faithful watch care of your joint assets and the place where you live will accomplish all this and more as you look to our dear Lord for His gracious enablement.

Money Should Matter to You

By agreeing with God about the importance of doing your best to manage your part of the family finances, and by making a commitment to Him to do a better job with *His* resources, money, and the wise management of it will begin to matter to you. Therefore you'll want to be sure you are...

- ☞ *Praying*—because managing God's money is not only a spiritual issue requiring spiritual disciplines and character qualities, but it is a matter of obedience.

- ☞ *Giving*—because God asks you to.

- ☞ *Saving*—because it will better your family. Save for your children's and grandchildren's educational funds. Save for a home or home furnishings. Save for retirement. Save for a special trip, vacation, or missions trip. Save, too, to fund someone's ministry.

- ☞ *Budgeting*—because a budget maps out the path for your lifestyle.

- ☞ *Doing without*—because a host of spiritual disciplines are birthed and enhanced as you do so.

- ☞ *Bewaring*—of greed, lust, bitterness, and envy.

- ☞ *Growing*—in contentment.

Mastering Your Money

Now that you understand more about God's guidelines and plan for your money, how can you begin to put them to work in your marriage? How can you begin to master your money...and your heart? Here's an initial list of "Things to Do."

    ☞   Present to God the firstfruits of all your income. That's the advice of Proverbs 3:9-10—"Honor the LORD with your possessions, and with the first-fruits of all your increase; so your barns will be filled with plenty, and your vats will overflow with new wine." Giving back to God paves the way for even greater blessing. Oh, please, don't give God your leftovers. Give Him the first...and the best.

    ☞   Put those communication skills to work! Talk over this area of your marriage with your husband. Take this book to your hubby and show him what you're learning about money management. Let him know you'd like to talk about it sometime. And by all means, be sweet, be patient, be wise. Rather than begin preaching and lecturing, ask what he thinks about what you've shared.

    ☞   Put some personal goals into motion. Whether or not your husband agrees to talk about, change, or take charge of the way you approach money management as a couple, you can personally make some changes. For instance, you can determine to shop less, to spend less, to work on a heart of contentment, to become a more skillful home manager, to live a simpler life, to be more prayerful and creative about taking care of your family's needs at home.

☞   Purchase a book about the financial in's and out's of home management. Let such a book teach you how to become a tightwad (in a good sense, that is)—how to save, how to cut spending, and how to manage your part of the household budget. This can only help your finances, and in no way takes away from your husband's leadership of the family.

Doing Your Part

I hope and pray the scriptures included in this chapter have helped to open your eyes—and heart!—to at least two primary ways you as a wife after God's own heart can put these biblical principles to work in your marriage and contribute on the "earning" end of the finances. First, you contribute much to your husband by the wise, thrifty, diligent management and oversight of your part of the household budget. And second, you contribute even

> *You contribute much to your marriage by the wise, thrifty, diligent management and oversight of your part of the household budget.*

more by heartily supporting your husband (versus nagging, whining, and complaining because he's always at work or always tired from the demands on his job) as he puts forth the effort—and the hours—to do his part in providing for your family.

Here's how I saw my daughter Courtney put this attitude to work in her marriage. On one particular visit Jim and I took to her home, Paul was in U.S. Navy submarine school from 6 A.M. (before the children woke up) to 10 P.M. (after the children were in bed) almost every day for a year. However, he did have a one-hour break for lunch. Subtracting time for Paul's trip home and back to his school meant Paul and Courtney and their two babies had 40 precious, golden minutes together every day at lunchtime.

Now, here's how Courtney handled this. First and most important, there was no nagging, whining, or complaining. Instead, Courtney blocked off every morning to cook a full-out meal, to carefully and beautifully set the table, to make sure the children were napped and rested, dressed, and as cheerful as possible, to bake homemade cookies, and see that a thermos full of strong coffee was set by the door. At 12:10 their squealing little family was standing at the front door to welcome "Daddy" home. Quickly the kids were hoisted into high chairs, prayers were offered to God, and everyone was treated to a gourmet meal at a gala table. When their 40 minutes were up, all lined up again at the door to kiss Daddy goodbye as Courtney handed Paul the thermos and a sackful of fresh cookies to help him make it through until ten o'clock.

Dear wife, this is the way it is (or is supposed to be!). You and I are to support our husbands as they support us. We grease the skids, so to speak, by making his life easier with our joy, support, encouragement, effort, creative planning, and wise scheduling. That's our job-assignment from God. Like the wise wife in Proverbs 31:12, we are to do our husbands "good and not evil all the days of [our] life." Then, in time, we reap a multitude of rewards. As I shared earlier, there was a period of time in my marriage when Jim worked practically all day and all night at four different jobs to provide for our family. In fact, for the 30-plus years he was in the Army Reserves, he had two jobs (and sometimes more). Our family reaped the benefits of Jim's hard work then, and we are reaping them now as our home mortgage is paid off and we are enjoying full medical benefits and some monthly income from his three decades of exertion on all of his many jobs. My thoughts go something like this, *Surely, if my husband is to provide, I can do my part by helping to make life easier for him in as many ways as I can.*

Now, don't you agree?

Heart Response

May I add one final principle here in our Heart Response section? Beloved wife after God's own heart, you and I must realize that in God's economy, *many things are more important than money.*

For instance, your *character* is more important than money—"Those who are of a perverse heart are an abomination to the LORD, but the blameless in their ways are His delight" (Proverbs 11:20). Your *reputation*, too, is better than money—"A good name is to be chosen rather than great riches" (Proverbs 22:1). *Wisdom* is also more important than money—"The crown of the wise is their riches" (Proverbs 14:24); "how much better to get wisdom than gold! And to get understanding is to be chosen rather than silver" (Proverbs 16:16). And *humility* is better than money—"By humility and the fear of the LORD are riches and honor and life" (Proverbs 22:4).

And here's another twist—*you*, as a godly wife, are better than money to your husband! "Houses and riches are an inheritance from fathers, but *a prudent wife* is from the LORD" (Proverbs 19:14). In fact, according to the Bible, *you*, as a godly wife, are your husband's greatest asset. With a godly wife of character, humility, wisdom, and faithfulness beside him, the Bible says your husband "will have no lack of gain" (Proverbs 31:11). Why? Because as "a virtuous wife" *your* "worth is far above rubies" (verse 10).

Little Things That Make a Big Difference

1. Honor your husband's direction.

Every husband handles finances differently. Your job is to learn how your husband wants the money managed. Would he rather you make purchases with cash, check, debit card, or credit card? Find out and then honor his desire. Also get into the habit of checking with him before you make purchases or order repairs. Your shopping, spending, and home improvements shouldn't be a secret mission, a covert operation, or a surprise. Ask him, show him, and inform him about your plans. Discuss Christmas and birthday gifts and spending allowances in advance. Go over any repairs or improvements you think are necessary. Always seek to know his wishes...and then honor them.

2. Create a budget.

Of course, the best scenario would be for you and your husband to create a budget together. But if he's not interested or too busy to think it through, make—and keep—one for the areas of the family finances where you are involved (food, household items, clothing, gifts). Follow these three steps in keeping a budget and become an expert at the financial management of those items in your daily sphere:

    ☞   *Determine*...a reasonable amount for each category

    ☞   *Record*...what you spend

    ☞   *Wait*...until the funds are available

3. Help out with managing the finances.

See how many ways you can help out with bill paying, recordkeeping, filing, and organizing. Ask your husband the best way you can assist him or lighten his burden in the family's Accounting Department. Is it keeping stamps on hand? Is it taking the bills to the post office? Is it learning how to use a computer program to keep track of expenses? Two sure ways to help out are to keep your checkbook up to date and to check your bank balance daily.

4. Set up a financial center.

Do you want to improve the money management around your home? Then organize all financial functions in one location by setting up a financial center. It doesn't have to be large or elaborate. Just a little table in the corner will do. Simply make sure everything you need is there: pens, pencils, a good lamp, stapler, stamps, envelopes, notepads, accordion folders for filing bills and receipts, maybe a two-drawer file cabinet with a box of file folders in one drawer...and, of course, a copy of your household budget. If you are really limited in space, you can keep everything in a portable plastic file box with a handle on it and move it from place to place.

5. Give to God's purposes.

In a feature article for couples entitled "What Draws Us Closer to God?" tithing and giving to the poor and needy were noted as two acts that not only draw a couple closer to one another but also to God.[3] Together you and your husband can decide where you want to focus your giving. Obviously, your church should be first. Then where? Realize that giving to your church and sharing with others breeds many wonderful qualities in you, your husband, and your family, and it blesses the lives of countless others.

6. Keep a list of things you want or need.

Every time something comes up that you want or need, jot it down on an ongoing list. Then, as with all lists, prioritize what you see according to desire or urgency. Also jot down an estimate of the cost or price of the items. As we noted in Little Thing #1, you'll want to share your list with your husband. Then use your "wish-and-want list" as a prayer list.

7. Set up a savings plan.

Again, the ideal would be for you and your husband to do this together. But if that doesn't work out, then see what you can do in the Savings Department.

Just having a savings plan will motivate you to cut corners, cut spending, and cut out coupons—whatever it takes to tuck some money away for emergencies or for family fun. And speaking of fun, consider keeping a piggy bank or money jar that you and your husband put all your change into every day for some fun purchase or trip. You'll be surprised how quickly savings will amass (and how much fun you'll have)!

6

Keeping Up the Home

Through wisdom a house is built,
and by understanding it is established;
by knowledge the rooms are filled
with all precious and pleasant riches.
PROVERBS 24:3-4

How is your home-sweet-home? And how's the atmosphere under your roof? As you and I both know, keeping up the home can be another source of tension in a marriage.

One day a young married friend phoned me at home and asked what she should do. She explained that she and her husband had purchased their first-ever home...which provided them with their first-ever lawn...and a new problem. She asked, "Mrs. George, what should I do? My husband works very hard, and when he gets home, he just doesn't seem to have the desire or the energy to mow the lawn. And he wants to relax on the weekends. Meanwhile our grass is getting higher and higher. I asked him if I could

mow it for him, and he said no, that it was his job. Several
weeks later I asked him if we could hire a gardener or a
teenager from the neighborhood to cut it, and again, the
answer was no, he would do it. And guess what? It's still
not done. I want to be submissive, but what can I do?"

My hat went off to this lovely young wife. And my heart
went out to her. She wanted to honor her husband, she
wanted to follow his wishes, she wanted to help him, and
she loved him. But an issue centered at and around the
home was becoming a real problem. What can a wife after
God's own heart do about keeping up the home where she
and her husband live?

God's Perspective on a Home

During the years that I've been reading through my
Bible, I've looked for scriptures relating to certain topics
that apply to my roles as a Christian woman, wife, mother,
and homemaker. Two of those topics are "time management" and "home." One day I hit the jackpot—a verse that
addressed both! It's a haunting verse concerning King
Hezekiah, the fifteenth king of Judah. As this man lay sick
and dying, God sent His prophet Isaiah with these words of
instruction: "Set your house in order, for you shall die, and
not live" (2 Kings 20:1). Given the historical time line of
this announcement in Israel's history, God was possibly
letting King Hezekiah know that he needed to not only
tend to his domestic and private affairs, but also to those
of the state of his kingdom.

But for me, the advice arrowed its way straight into my heart as a homemaker. *I* needed to set my house in order, to see to the affairs in *my* home.

Did you know that your home is important, not only to you and your husband and children, but to God? In fact, God has a great deal to say about your home, homemaking, and home management.

You are to "build" your home. That's what the wise wife does. "The wise woman builds her house" (Proverbs 14:1). One sourcebook points out that the unique combination of the words "woman" and "house" and the reference to "wisdom" place this verse with four other scriptures that translate "mother's house," a term for the family household. Such a term "reflects a woman's perspective and also expresses female agency in managing an agrarian household in ancient Israel." The scholars add, "The link here with wisdom adds the dimension of female technological expertise and sagacity to the managerial aspects of senior women in family life."[1] In short, a woman of wisdom views taking care of her house as an important role and priority in her life. And she manages her home, property, and household with wisdom, expertise, and intelligence.

> *A dedicated homemaker keeps a keen eye over all that goes on in her home.*

Now let me share the second half of Proverbs 14:1. While the wise woman is busy building her house, "the foolish pulls it down with her hands." This means that while the wise wife is painstakingly pouring her efforts into building her house and increasing its wealth, the foolish wife is lessening its value by mismanagement.[2]

Are you, dear homemaker, building up your home...or are you breaking it down?

You are to watch over your home. That's what the ideal wife we looked at earlier did. "She watches over the ways of her household, and does not eat the bread of idleness" (Proverbs 31:27). Therefore as wives after God's own heart, you and I should follow heartily in her footsteps. After all, she's God's ideal wife. Here is a diligent, careful, energetic, and dedicated homemaker who keeps a keen eye over all that goes on in her home, both with the people and the place. *How,* we wonder, *did she do it?* God gives us the answer: She "does not eat the bread of idleness." In other words, she is "not content to go through life eating and sleeping...and is never lazy."[3] Shallow, unproductive activities have no place in her life. Why, she's on assignment from God to keep watch over the affairs of her household!

How's your eye? Is its gaze fixed at home?

And how are your efforts? Are they focused on the place where you live?

And how's your energy level? Where do you register when it comes to the Eating and Sleeping Department versus the Never-Lazy Department? Are you giving your all—your every minute—to building your home-sweet-home?

You are to manage your home. There's some history behind this management aspect of your homemaking. You see, the apostle Paul did not want the young widows in the early church to "be idle, wandering about from house to house, and not only idle but also gossips and busybodies, saying things which they ought not." Instead he desired that they "marry, bear children, *manage the house*" (1 Timothy 5:13-14). There are several principles here we can draw out for all wives. First, it is a good thing to have a home to manage. Paul definitely saw managing a home as better than being lazy, a gad-about, a gossip, and a busybody. But second, a wife is to "manage" her house. Taking care of and guiding the work that goes into making a house a home is a good thing.

You are to keep your home. This principle for all married women who desire to follow after God comes from Titus 2:5. Here considerable emphasis is placed on the foundation of the home, and the older women in the church are instructed to spend their time teaching the younger women to, among other things, be homemakers. The message to you and me today, as well as to the women of Titus' day, is that we are to spend our time in our own homes being the "guardians of the house."[4] And how is this done? The oldest manuscripts convey the answer in their translations: We are to be "workers at home," "active in household duties."[5] In other words, we are to be doing the work it takes to make a house a home.

As a bonus in our understanding, three other scriptures teach the same principle. Two of them will sound familiar. And be on guard—two of them are taught from the negative, pointing to the woman who does *not* take care of her home.

- Proverbs 7:11-12—These verses describe, of all things, an adulteress. She is doing the opposite of the wise homemaker who tends to her house and housework. She is "out there," walking the streets, instead of being at home. "Her feet would not stay at home. At times she was outside, at times in the open square, lurking at every corner."

- Proverbs 14:1—One scholar translates this now-familiar verse as "wisdom builds the house of life: frivolity pulls it down."[6] Spending her precious time on frivolous things, the home of the foolish woman is not only *not* "built," but it is actually destroyed.

- 1 Timothy 5:13-14—Once again, this verse calls us to analyze what we are doing and where we are spending our time and effort when we are not at home taking care of our business there.

I don't know about you, but I love to know what God says and what God wants from me. Knowing helps me to understand why something is important because I can then whole-heartedly roll up my sleeves, look to God for His divine enablement, dive in, and do it. With these few principles for homemaking to guide us as wives and home-makers after God's own heart, we can certainly better understand our role in the vital area of marriage of keeping up the home.

Problems and Solutions

However, here's what I found to be true. Once I determined to dive in, I immediately encountered a few problems. Do you relate to any of them? Are you plagued by any on this list?

I'm so tired! (And what woman isn't?) Tiredness is a fact of life. Therefore, I approach my every day and my whole life as a quest for energy. I am doggedly trying to discover how to gain energy, how to sustain it, how to ensure it, and how to boost it. I study my energy levels, down to what kind of response the food I eat has on my body and mind. I chart my peak energy times and note the not-so-peak ones.

And here's something else I've learned. When I am the most tired is when I need to do whatever it takes to get myself moving. My son-in-law is a physics teacher, and he shared the following Law of Physics with me: A body at rest tends to remain at rest, and a body in motion tends to remain in motion.

Solutions—Try your hand at paying attention to and recording your energy levels. And while you're at it, try to put your finger on what may have contributed to a burst of energy or to a drop in your momentum. Also pick one activity you will willfully participate in when you feel like you simply cannot continue on or keep moving. This is usually when I turn on the *Headline News* and begin rinsing out dishes, loading or unloading the dishwasher, and wiping off counters. Sometimes I peel carrots or potatoes, or measure and rinse rice and get it into the rice cooker. I willfully make the effort on some no-brainer activity. Amazingly, such a small exertion gets me going again...or keeps me going. As one of my life mottos says, "Something is always better than nothing" no matter how small that "something" is.

And here's a big "something"—Do whatever you have to do to get your rest. I know it sounds impossible, but you must work on it. For me, I try to head for the bedroom around seven o'clock. I don't go to bed then, but I can start on my bedtime rituals, take another look at my planner, go through the junk mail, turn through magazines, and take care of a plethora of other little odd jobs...and all from my wonderful bed! This practice helps me get to bed one to two hours earlier than I would if I kept puttering or lazing around downstairs and translates into one to two hours of additional sleep per night. So what can you do to get to bed earlier so that you get more rest? Eliminate some evening television? Cut your caffeine intake? Get the children into bed earlier?

I have so many children! I can't help but think of "the old woman who lived in a shoe," who had so many children she didn't know what to do! But, truthfully, I meet many women who have between six and ten children. And, truthfully, *any* number of children presents a new set of demands on *any* woman and couple.

Solutions—Here's another principle that guides my life in every area every day. It's my version of a Law of Economics: "When something goes up, something else must go down." For instance, when the two of you—you and your husband—get your life into a groove, and then a baby is added, something has to give, has to be eliminated or set aside, has to go down. Then, as additional children are added, more and more things have to go. Why? Because something more important (to you and to God—see Genesis 1:28 and Psalm 127:3-5)—precious children—has come to take the place of lesser things, even frivolous things. For me, with two little ones only 13 months apart, night classes had to go. Also my little "running around" capers had to be pared down to one morning per week. And suddenly my telephone time had to be cut way down because it seemed like my washing machine was "calling" me as it worked overtime taking care of the mountains of little pieces of laundry that had to also be folded and put away.

Determining what you trim out of your life to make time for caring for your God-given children will be something you and your husband decide together. You'll want to be in agreement so you are operating from a solid base and the same set of principles. So, once again, sharpen up those communication skills and put them to work for you as the two of you seek God's will and what is best for your family.

I don't know what to do! Which translates, I lack time management skills. Perhaps in your heart you are crying out, "Yes, I want to do it. I want to keep up my home." But at the same time you are wondering, "But how am I supposed to manage my time and my tasks? What do I do first, how does one plan, and how in the world does one attack a project?"

Solution—Good news! Management skills can be learned. I am a living, breathing, walking testimony to this truth. If you desire it, you can learn it. How? By asking your husband. By asking others. By taking classes. By reading books. By using good planning tools and calendars. But I warn you, it will take time—time each day as well as a lifetime. Thirty years ago I discovered this adage to be true: "Life is what happens to you while you're failing to plan it." And I woke up one day with a husband and two babies and didn't know what to do. *Life* had happened.

So I started asking for help, taking the classes, reading the books, using a planner—all in a quest to learn how to manage my time and my good housekeeping projects. And, lest you think I've arrived, I'm still learning. I've grown a lot, but I'm still asking productive people for better ways of getting things done. I'm still reading (although I already own ten feet of time management books on my bookshelves). I'm still listening when others give a seminar or have a tape or CD available. I'm still on the lookout for a better planner and organizational system. And I hope you are doing the same.

I don't know how! Now that you've ordered your projects, put your plans on paper, know where to start and what to do, your next dilemma is *how* to do it. This is a clear case of lacking homemaking skills.

Solution—Good news again! Expertise in taking care of your home can also be learned. And once again I am a living, breathing, walking testimony to this fact. Here's where godly, older women come in. According to Titus 2:3-5, these ladies are to be available and actively teaching the in's and out's of being a wife after God's own heart to their younger sisters-in-Christ. And the curriculum includes the area of homemaking skills (verse 5). So see if you can latch on to one of these dear saints! Pray, ask for help, and then try doing what you are being taught.

Again, this will require time—time meeting with another woman, time each day as you keep up your home, and time for a lifetime as you obtain your skills, perfect them, improve them, and use them. But, oh, will it be worth it! What better place or way could you be spending the precious time God gives you than by working out His will right under your own roof, than by blessing your husband and family by your loving efforts at home?

I don't care! Oh dear! I hope this isn't true of you because this is the worst of all the "problems"...and the one that no one can fix or help unless the owner of such an attitude has a change of heart. And it's the most scary of all the scenarios because it is a *spiritual* problem. You see, you and I can know that we should take care of and keep up our homes, and we can know that we need to do it. We can know that our husbands would appreciate it and desire our assistance in this area. We can even know that God wants us to do it—but still we just plain ole don't care to do it.

Solution—This "problem" falls into a completely different category than the others. This is not a problem of ignorance, busyness, or physical tiredness. No, in the case of an I-don't-care-attitude, we are facing a sin issue. A rebellious spirit. A cold-hearted decision to say, think, and act with the attitude of *So what?* and *I don't care!*

Someone has written that "the honor of the Word of God is the supreme sanction for right conduct."[7] And, as Titus 2:5 states, after instructing us to be "homemakers," you and I are to do so in order "that the word of God may not be blasphemed." In other words, we are to follow God's instructions so that our behavior in no way dishonors, defames, maligns, discredits, scandalizes, or causes suffering to the Word of God and the gospel of Jesus Christ.

As you can see, a defiant attitude toward God's will and God's Word is most serious. I love a line of poetry that suggests, "Little one, search that heart of thine."[8] And now I'm asking you to do just that—to search your heart and, as David prayed, "see if there is any wicked way in me" (Psalm 139:24). If there is, I beg you to confess it, forsake it, and, with God's help, change your mind-set regarding your home. God wants you, as one of His women, to become a better steward of your home. Don't miss out on the blessing of a happy home!

I have a job! More and more women enter the workforce each year. And if you fall into the category of women who must tend to a job on top of tending to their homefront, it will help to follow a few guiding principles. I've devoted Chapter 9 to this subject, and it's filled with solutions to this real-life issue. But for now, look at the chapter titles on the Contents page. They represent "things that really make a difference in your marriage." Every one of these areas of a wife's life must be nursed. Each is a stewardship handed to us from the heart and mind of God. Each is according to His wisdom and His will. This list provides us with

> *We are called to set aside "self" and do the work of building a home where love reigns and order prevails.*

God-assigned duties and responsibilities. And, as the Bible says, it is required of a steward that he or she be found faithful (1 Corinthians 4:2).

Heart Response

As I pause to survey the past 30 years of seeking to be a wife according to God's plan, how I thank Him for His desire for me to be a homemaker! And how I thank Him for what He has graciously worked into me as I've pursued His desire—the skills, the character qualities, the confidence of being in His will, doing His will, and, hopefully and prayerfully, doing it well. And how I am humbled that keeping up my home is a way that I can bring honor and glory to Him. And how I praise Him that, in some small ways, I have grown in Christlikeness as I have learned to serve my husband and children under our roof, to set aside "self" and do the work (although it is a labor of love) of building a home where love reigns and order prevails. Of course, there have been the failures, the squabbles, the bloops and blunders. But through it all, there is no blessing like that of a happy home. Now, dear fellow homemaker, take the challenging words that follow to heart. And as you focus your energies on keeping up your home, may yours be a happy one enjoying the blessing of God.

> Six things are requisite to create a "happy home."
> *Integrity* must be the architect, and
> *Tidiness* the upholsterer. It must be warmed by
> *Affection*, lighted up with
> *Cheerfulness;* and
> *Industry* must be the ventilator, renewing the atmo-
> sphere and bringing in fresh [vitality] day by day;
> while over all, as a protecting canopy and glory,
> nothing will suffice except
>
> *The blessing of God.*[9]

Little Things That Make a Big Difference

1. Make the beds daily.

This is truly the definition of a little thing! After all, what does it take to make a bed, maybe two minutes? Even if there is clutter in other places in a bedroom, a smooth, wrinkle-free bed gives the appearance of order and serenity. Of course, you'll want to get to that clutter one of these days. But make bed-making a daily habit. And if you have children, have them do the same.

2. Make a daily to-do list.

Start keeping up your home in this small, simple, time-tested way. Make a to-do list. Write down what you hope or need to get done each day that will enhance your home and family life. Go a step further and star or circle the most important one. Then, of course, do it! As you begin to master this little thing, you'll want to begin working on a master plan for caring for your home that includes...

...a weekly plan,   ...a semi-annual plan,

...a monthly plan,   ...an annual plan.[10]

...a quarterly plan,

3. Make a weekly meal menu.

For the smooth running of any household, a menu ensures that you and your loved ones eat (...and, as the old adage promises, the way to a man's heart is through his stomach!). So begin by making your menu for one week at a time. This allows you to have some special meals, some fast meals, and some made with leftovers. A menu also means you only go to the grocery store once a week. And here's another little thing—prepare as much of the evening meal as you can first thing in the morning. Our days certainly have a way of slipping away from us, don't they? And when yours does, you still have a meal to put on the table...all because you started early.

4. Do one thing you've been putting off.

What is the one thing you've been putting off around your house that, if you did it, would give you tremendous relief and great joy? Is it organizing the master bedroom closet? Is it cleaning out the refrigerator? Is it washing the windows? Is it sorting through the junk in the garage? Even if you only work on your project 15 minutes a day, your rewards will be large!

5. Keep a daily log of time spent on your housework.

This is very simple. Several times a day, jot down an estimate of the total number of minutes you've invested in any and all household chores. Your time log doesn't have to be exact or to the minute. What you are looking for is a record that will give you an idea of how much time you are actually devoting to your home-sweet-home. And one picture is worth a thousand words! If the truth reveals that your actual time is low, then you can make plans to put in a little more time and effort each day.

6. Work on your attitude.

Long before the seven dwarfs were whistling while they worked, God addressed the importance of a good attitude toward work. *How* do we work? "Heartily, as to the Lord and not to men" (Colossians 3:23) and "willingly" (Proverbs 31:13). Therefore, a wife after God's own heart does her best in her work at home. She works with a positive attitude. She works to the glory of God (Martin Luther said a dairy maid could milk cows to the glory of God!). She works to better the lives of her loved ones. And she works with all her heart! How's your attitude?

7. Work on growing.

Once you get into keeping up your home, you'll be so blessed by the wonderful results that you'll begin taking pride in the place where you and your husband live. Then you'll want to learn new skills, new organizational methods, and new time management principles. So read, read, read! Ask your organized friends for recommendations of their favorite books on keeping up their home. Look for ways to constantly improve your work. You'll be glad you did...and so will your husband!

7

Raising Your Children

And these words which I command you
today shall be in your heart.
You shall teach them diligently to your children.
DEUTERONOMY 6:6-7

I have been asked again and again to write a book on
child-raising. In fact, I've even been asked to write
such a book with my two daughters, who are now raising
their own children. But honestly, I in no way feel like the
great parenting expert. As I look back down that rocky
path, I shudder. So many mistakes. So many failures. And,
praise be to God, also so much of His great and overwhelming grace!

Nothing, in my opinion and experience, is more hum-
bling than being a mother. When I think of a marriage, I
think of two adults. With your husband, you can at least
work on your communication skills and learn and adjust
your methods and means of transmitting and receiving
information. But with children? Well, all is different. You

are dealing with a baby...who becomes a child, a youth, an adolescent, a young adult, an adult. And the rules for living with and communicating with offspring at their varying ages and stages are...well...different. And here's where a great challenge comes in.

Parenting 101

I don't know where you are on the Parenting Scale. Perhaps you have no children...and, then again, perhaps you have a handful. Maybe yours are all little toddlers who are crawling on the floor, clamoring, and pulling on your legs all at the same time. Or possibly yours are in school—even high school. Or perhaps, like me, God has sent you into Round 2 and yours are your grandchildren. Whatever the case or age level, God is giving you an assignment like no other. While specific techniques for child-raising will come, go, and change, there are certain core values and fundamental practices that won't. As we go through some guidelines I am calling "Parenting 101," keep in mind that I am moving us in a natural progression from no children to grandchildren.

1. *Desire them*—It helps a wife to know *and believe* each and every day of her married life that children are a good thing. This teaching on the value of children and their place in God's perfect plan for a couple comes from Genesis 1:28. Here God commanded the two members of the first-ever marriage to "be fruitful and multiply," to "fill the earth." God also said "children are a heritage from the

LORD" and "the fruit of the womb is a reward." He concludes, "Happy is the man who has his quiver full of them" (Psalm 127:3,5).

Hannah in the Old Testament hoped desperately for children. Sarah, too, longed for them. So did Rebekah, Rachel, Manoah's wife, Elizabeth…and the list of women in the Bible who desired children stretches on.

I know children come to us in many ways and means, some initially more pleasant and joyful than others. But the assignment God gives to you as a woman and mother after His own heart is to pray fervently and seek to have His heart-attitude and mind-set toward the children who will or do make up your family.

2. *Pray to have them*—Hannah desired children so fiercely that she prayed to have them. In fact, her desire was so intense that she took her prayers to another level and made a vow to God (1 Samuel 1:10-11). The godly mother of Proverbs 31 appears to have also prayed and possibly made a vow. She referred to her son as not only the son of her womb, but as the "son of my vows" (verse 2).

So, dear friend, is the category "children" somewhere near the top of your prayer list? Whether you have children or not, that is their rightful place as you talk each day over with God through prayer.

Even to this day, on my own prayer list my children and grandchildren appear as third, right behind my walk with God and my relationship with Jim. They are "tops" in my heart and in my prayers!

3. *Welcome them*—When any and all babies arrive, realize that they are not the *end* of your life. Oh, no! They are the *beginning!* In fact, *they*—the next generation—are life itself. I love Sarah's attitude. First, when she heard that she just might (at age 90!) finally become a mother for the first time, she marveled, "After I have grown old, shall I have *pleasure*…?" (Genesis 18:12). In other words, Sarah was *thrilled* that she might have a child! Then, when she welcomed her little Isaac, she as much as sang in complete wonder, "God has made me laugh, and all who hear will laugh with me" (Genesis 21:6).

4. *Take them to church*—Once you hold your little newborns in your arms, begin their religious training in and for the Lord. On Day One of their little lives, start pointing them toward God. And on each baby's first Sunday as a member of your family, begin taking him or her regularly to church. Also, if your church has some kind of baby dedication ceremony, participate whole-heartedly. Mary took baby Jesus to the Temple at eight days old to fulfill a ritual required by God's Old Testament law (Luke 2:21) and again at 40 days old (verse 22). So follow suit, dear mom. Begin early to impress upon your heart and your infant's heart the importance of the Lord and the Lord's Day. Your tiny ones should never *not* know about God and His Son— your Savior—Jesus Christ. Beloved, devoted mom, it's

> *It's never too early to begin pointing your little ones' souls heavenward.*

never too early to begin pointing your little ones' souls heavenward…but it can subtly become too late. Please, don't wait!

5. *Love them*—Of course you love your family. But you must also pray each day for a heart of love. Why? Because as mothers we get tired. And many days we get so tired that we seem stretched to the limit. And the more children we have, the more tired we become. It's a given. What mother couldn't use a good night's sleep—regardless of how old her children are? But we are to love our children (rather than resent them, complain about them, grow impatient with them, desire to get away from them).

And we are to go a step further and express that love to God, to our children, and to others. I have to tell you that I cried when my daughter Katherine told me she fell apart and bawled her heart out when she left her little firstborn, Taylor Jane, for the first time to attend a women's retreat. (And Taylor was already 18 months old!) I cried because I cherish and share the heart of love that Katherine's tears indicated. And I cried, too, because I've been the speaker at many such women's retreats where the moms in attendance openly expressed how they couldn't wait to get away from their children. Actually, they called their God-given children "the brat-pack," "rug rats," and "the little monster." They wanted some "me" time, some "down" time, some space.

Please don't get me wrong. I understand the tensions, strains, wear-and-tear, and the toll the constancy of child-raising can have on a mom. After all, I've been one. But I do also believe our actions—and our mouths—betray our hearts more than we think. So, how high is your love quotient? Exactly what is your heart-attitude toward your role of mother and toward your children? Pray to love them, to love being with them, and to love being a mother—that's the whole point of the Bible's teaching and calling to wives and mothers "to *love* their children" (Titus 2:4).

6. *Teach them*—Look now at the scriptures at the beginning of this chapter. They are from God's law in Deuteronomy 6:6-7, and they tell you, as a parent after God's own heart, exactly what you are supposed to do every day of your life. You are to...

   ...teach your children

   ...teach God's Word

   ...teach diligently

   ...teach daily

These instructions from the heart of God show us that you and I are to teach our children, no matter what their ages. We are to teach them God's Word formally and purposefully. We are to teach them about God informally by talking about Him all day long, at every opportunity throughout the day, from the child's waking moment until he or she drops off to sleep. We are to impart information from the Bible itself, and we are to teach our children about God and godly living through everyday life experiences.

Can you tell that teaching your children requires that *you* love God and His Word and that you love your children? And can you tell that teaching your children requires time? Time every day? Time for a lifetime?

7. *Train them*—You and your husband (who is hopefully involved) are God's first choice for training your children. Yes, the church helps. So, perhaps, does a Christian school or preschool. And so do grandparents and other relatives. But God clearly assigns the training of children to those children's parents. Proverbs 1:8 specifically states, "My son, hear *the instruction of your father,* and do not forsake *the law of your mother*." Your job, dear mother after God's own heart, is to teach your children godly character qualities and godly ways. It is your assignment from your heavenly Father to teach and train your sons and daughters to respect others, to share, to be kind, to handle money properly, to work at a job, to be honest, to stay pure (see the parental training and instruction of Proverbs 5 and 7), and so on. Obviously, as their ages go up, the intensity of the subject matter goes up. But each and every step along the way matters. Don't skip, pass over, avoid, downplay, or take for granted any teaching that relates to your children's whole life experience.

Let's purpose to follow in the faithful, dedicated footsteps of the God-honoring mother of Proverbs 31:1-9. This woman's wise, grown son wrote, "The words of King Lemuel, the utterance which his mother taught him" (verse 1). Mom, this man had preserved the wise counsel that his *mother* taught him! And what, pray tell, was the essence of the teaching he shared in verses 1-9? First, his mother warned her son to avoid a life of dissipation and sensual lust. Second, she pleaded with him to refrain from the excessive use of wine and strong drink. Not bad advice, is it? And is it ever practical! As she prepared, groomed, and launched her son into manhood, this devoted mother spoke up from her heart. She poured out her love in the form of impassioned teaching in an effort to save her beloved son from future problems, harm, and ruin.

Now, I just had two thoughts of application. First, to participate in and accomplish all of this training, you, dear mom, must *be there*, as in be at home. And second, you must *be aware* of each child's development, tendencies, shortcomings, and strengths, not to mention how he or she spends time...and with whom. "Even a child is known by his deeds, whether what he does is pure and right" (Proverbs 20:11). How are you doing on these two requirements?

8. *Guide them*—Once your children are older and more "on their own" (off to college, out of the house, or working away from home on a summer job), you can still guide them by staying in touch and talking about the concerns of their lives and the decisions they are having to make. Samson discussed his desire to marry with his parents (Judges 14:1-4). Plus, there is much indication that the wise son, King Lemuel, who recorded his mother's advice in Proverbs 31:1-9, also followed her advice for selecting a wife (verses 31:10-31). As a godly parent, you are now—and always will be—a God-given asset to your children,

whatever their ages. So don't be afraid to offer your wisdom and advice.

9. *Befriend them*—Once your little ones have run the gamut and graduated to adulthood, you want to move quickly and naturally into the friendship category. Yes, you are still a most capable teacher, trainer, coach, cheerleader, confidante, counselor, and guide. But you now have the privilege and crowning joy of becoming your son's or daughter's adult friend. And what do we women do in the case of our friends? We stay in touch. We call, we talk, we send cards, emails, and little gifts. Our home is always open. And our hearts (of loving care), shoulders (to cry on or lean on), and arms (to hold) are always available.

If you are a mother of adult children, I beg you, don't hold back. Let them know they are important to you in as many ways as you can. Let them know, too, that they are even more important to you than your best friends. I well remember calling my parents when I was a college student to let them know I was homesick and wanted to come see them for a weekend visit. Can you imagine the blow of being told that it wasn't a good weekend because they were scheduled to play bridge with their friends? I got the message, loud and clear, that playing cards with another couple was more important to them than I was. What message are you sending to your adult children? Is it one of cherished best-friendship?

10. *Mates? Welcome them!*—We'll deal with expanding and extended family in the next chapter. But for now, just

file this away—It is vitally important that you welcome your son's and daughter's mates into your heart when they marry. You must bond and meld, for you see, once they are married, you are "family"! In the case of our two daughters, Jim and I approached their courtships and engagements with a cool reserve, knowing that anything can happen to a couple right up to the second they walk down the aisle, even to and through the exchange of wedding vows. But I have to tell you that once Katherine and Courtney walked back up the aisle on the arm of their new (and for real) husbands, those men were mine. Both Pauls (yes, each daughter married a Paul!) instantly became, in my heart, not merely sons-in-law, but sons—*my* sons. They are the sons I never had...the sons God gave to me through marriage. I would gladly die for either one of them.

And what happens after the activity and frenzy of the wedding ceremony? Your adult married children must leave you and their childhood home (Genesis 2:24) and cleave to their mates. But they need to know of your utter joy and delight. And they need your understanding, support, love, prayers, and encouragement.

Jim and I got to express this support in an unusual way. One evening we hosted one of our newlywed couples for a dinner at our home. During conversation, my daughter casually stated while we were eating, "Oh, I would never move away from you, Mom and Dad!" Now, how did we encourage her? Selfishly, these words were music to our ears. But we soon talked to her privately and reminded her of the leaving and cleaving aspect in marriage, that her role was to follow her husband as he provided for her. Jim and I want what's best for our girls and their Pauls, and God's best requires that we let go and give our young families freedom to pursue God's best for them, and, of course, to love and pray for them and to visit as often as we can....

11. *Grandchildren? Welcome them!*—Surely you can see that the cycle of family life continues on and on and on. Some things never change, and one of those things is the heart of a mother. I have a confession to make. I am the grandmother of five little tykes, all four and under, and I can hardly wait until they marry and have their own babies and place them into my arms. I can't wait to welcome a third generation and begin this cycle of praying, loving, teaching, training, and befriending all over again, Lord willing. Oh, what joy that will be! What fulfillment! What answers to a lifetime of prayers! What praise to God! And what a new responsibility!

12. *Pray for them*—And now we start the sequence all over again! What is a mother? She is a woman who prays for her children, their mates, and their children. Perhaps being a prayer is her first and finest role in life. She is the one who is always praying... and her children know it. And now, just as you prayed before your children were conceived, prayed when they were conceived, prayed when

> *What is a mother? She is a woman who prays for her children. Perhaps that is her first and finest role in life.*

they were born, when they were preschoolers, grade schoolers, junior high schoolers, high schoolers, and college students or in the workforce, you continue to pray for them now...and forever. Such a life of prayer and dedicated prayer effort on behalf of our precious children is "the very highest energy of which the mind is capable."[1]

Heart Response

When it comes to what God's Word tells us about being wise and godly mothers, I have to first tell you that I have written my heart out on this subject in almost every book I've written. Why? Because any Christian woman who has children, stepchildren, or grandchildren, has an important duty and responsibility before God concerning those children *He* has placed in her life. And now, in yet another book, I'm humbly addressing the topic of godly parenting and the awesome role of being a mother again. And I have to report to you that my heart is pounding as I am freshly reminded through the Scriptures of what an overwhelming, life-consuming, life-long priority raising children is for a woman after God's own heart. I'm back on my knees, feeling inadequate (which I most definitely am without God's gracious assistance!). And, once again, I'm looking to our all-powerful, all-wise, all-caring God who promises that "with Him all things are possible" (see Matthew 19:26)— even the impossible task of godly parenting.

So do as I'm doing...

Acknowledge the role God has given you.

Commit afresh to live out that role...by His grace.

Make every effort to follow through.

Pray even more fervently, frequently, and faithfully!

Little Things That Make a Big Difference

1. Have a schedule.

Notice I didn't say *follow* a schedule! That's next to impossible for the mom in a busy household. But at the same time, every wise mother has a daily schedule and routine. If you want your day to run more flawlessly, begin with a plan in mind. Schedule meal times, nap times, play times, errand time, bath time, and bed time. As much as is possible, stick to your schedule. Be strong and say *no* to deviations. Your goal is to get your children into a groove so they expect to do certain things, in a specific order, and at certain times. Also plan in time for your housework. And plan in a breather for yourself. Of course there will be the odd day out (errands, Bible study), but your children will pick up on and welcome the general pattern you set for their days. Even if you have a job, you can still schedule and create a morning and evening routine that gives your family a sense of structure, normalcy, and home.

2. Get up before the children do.

Speaking of schedules, this one's for you, dear mom—You must beat the children up! By this I mean you must get up before the rest of the family does. Getting up after they do is a form of suicide.

You start your day behind, and guess what? You never catch up! So what happens when you get up a little earlier? You have time to officially wake up, sit quietly alone, read from the Bible, make your to-do list for the day, and pray for your day and your dear family. You'll be a better mom for it.

3. Set up a recreational area.

When your children have an exciting, inviting place to play or be creative, it centers them at home. Boredom dwindles because there are so many things to do and a place to do them. This is a "little thing," but it makes for happier, more active children. Plus, as an added bonus, it streamlines everyone's task of picking up (which you've scheduled in three times a day—before lunch, before Daddy comes home, and before bedtime, right?). Everything is in one room or one place. You can have cubbyholes or lockers or boxes or baskets for each child to put his or her things into. You can have a general storage area (cubbyhole, locker, box, basket, or closet shelf) for general art supplies, craft items, musical instruments, or audio/video/computer equipment. Sounds like a fun place to me!

4. Have a daily instruction time.

While you are making a schedule and creating a routine for your family, plan in a daily instruction time. This is a time when *every* child who is still at home during the day can sit around your breakfast, dining, or Ping-Pong table and receive some hands-on instruction from Mom. You can set up a craft. You can have the children work a lesson in a workbook or sticker-book designed to help them with their alphabet, shapes, and numbers. You can work with flash cards. You can play a teaching or story tape for their age level. Just be sure each child sits in a chair (or high chair!) and has something structured to work on that's age-appropriate. Make it a little bit formal, a whole lot of fun, and be sure you pray when you begin. We all need God's help when it comes to learning!

5. Have a daily Bible time with Mom.

While you are making a schedule and creating a routine for your family, plan in a daily Bible time. This is not an instructional time, but an enjoyable time, as reading the Bible should always be. This is when you pause for a snack, pile on the couch with Mom in the middle, and have cookies and milk while Mom (or an older child) reads from the Bible, a rhyming Bible, or a Bible storybook. Make it fun, warm, and cozy—something *very* special that all of you get to do together. Afterward, have everyone pray a sentence prayer relating to the Bible story. Then, of course, when Daddy gets home, have the children tell him what they read about in their Bible time. Start with the wonderful stories of Jesus, the action heroes-of-faith from the Old Testament, and the tales and adventures of the apostle Paul. Be sure the Bible is a part of your children's everyday life—no matter what their ages!

8

Extending Love to Family

If it is possible, as much as depends on you,
live peaceably with all men.
ROMANS 12:18

The penalty for bigamy is two mothers-in-law.

The wife isn't always boss in the American home. Sometimes it's her mother.

To the average husband, the "blessed event" is when his mother-in-law goes home.

"Double trouble" is a mother-in-law with a twin sister.

These one-liners make gentle fun of mothers-in-law, but the good news is that these quips don't reflect everyone's experience. And, dear reader, as a Christian woman—a woman after God's own heart—they *shouldn't* reflect your relationship with your mother-in-law...or with any of your extended family.

What bliss it was for Jim and me as an engaged couple to finally get married. After all of the courting, planning, preparing, and the wedding, off we went on our honeymoon with stars in our eyes and an abundance of love and joy in our hearts.

But after the wedding, real life arrived. It was then Jim and I realized that as a couple we were a new unit, and that each of us came with a full-blown family attached. We now had new issues to deal with. For instance, which set of parents were we going to spend time with first? How often should we get together with our parents? Should we use our hard-earned money (of which there was never enough!) to travel far distances to visit out-of-state parents and in-laws? What about those brothers and sisters who had been our best friends since childhood? And how should we deal with the strain we sometimes feel in these relationships?

God's Perfect Plan

Well, thank the Lord that for every problem He has a solution—a *divine* solution. And in the case of family problems, God has help for His couples. We've already looked at God's plan for newlyweds to "leave" their parents and "cleave" to their spouses (Genesis 2:24). Once a "child" is raised and married, God means for that offspring and his or her mate to form a new union separate and apart from their parents. God also plans for the marriage to be indissoluble—to be Super Glued together ("glue" being the literal meaning of the word "cleave")—until death parts the partners.

God's perfect plan of leaving and cleaving places a two-fold responsibility on all members of the husband's and wife's families. First, the parents on both sides are to voluntarily step out of their "child's" life and release their hold on their adult child. They are to bless the new couple's union through marriage, support them, encourage them, and above all, pray for them. The first years of a marriage are rocky enough without adding the tension of in-law problems. And the second responsibility is that of the newly formed couple to step away and out of their family home and circle. You see, each family must divide before it can multiply.

It's like a dance. The young couple has to step away, and the family units need to let them do so. And yet, once the new twosome has stepped out, they are to step back in. They are still family, but the flavor of the family takes on a new mix. Each family unit has changed in that the married adult child now has a partner—a soul-mate, a one-flesh relationship and friendship with someone else. And it is the two-become-one that returns to each former family unit to strengthen and better that unit as a family is extended, multiplied, and promoted by a new generation. In the end, God has made each family become two—two units that are friends and dedicated to one another, two units that love and cherish one another and gladly invite the other into their hearts.

And God has other plans for His couples. Read on!

The First Law with a Promise

Everyone loves a promise, especially if that promise promotes quality of life. And God has a promise for you and me *if* we follow the law that He laid down with it. I'm referring to one of God's laws as handed down in the Ten Commandments. Commandment #5 states, "Honor your father and your mother, that your days may be long upon the land which the LORD your God is giving you" (Exodus 20:12). An adult is obligated to honor his parents as he does God and to assume responsibility for them.

> *God asks for obedience to His command to honor parents, and He promises a spiritually blessed life to the one who obeys.*

This "law" is also repeated in the New Testament. In the book of Ephesians we read, "'Honor your father and mother,' which is the first commandment with promise: 'that it may be well with you and you may live long on the earth'" (Ephesians 6:2-3). In other words, God asks for obedience to His command to honor parents, and He promises a spiritually blessed life on the way to the higher blessing of eternal life.

Love Lived Out

In the daughter-in-law/mother-in-law combination of Ruth and Naomi, we see God's Law of Honor and Blessing and Love lived out. These two wives after God's own heart make up the Bible's classic study of a God-honoring in-law relationship.

What happened to bring them together? A *marriage* happened. Ruth married Naomi's son, and the two women became family. As we join them now, both of their husbands have died. They are two lone widows, each of whom has no one else for support or sustenance. Let's see what you as a wife can learn from their relationship that can be applied to yours with your in-laws. And as you read, keep in mind that the same principles apply to your relationship with your own parents. So seek to apply them all around—to your ties with mother and mother-in-law and with father and father-in-law. God is showing you how to honor your parents, whether they be parents or parents-in-law.

Ruth respected her mother-in-law—The words of Ruth's impassioned pledge of loyalty shout her respect for her mother-in-law and express unlimited love:

> Entreat me not to leave you, or to turn back from following after you; for wherever you go, I will go; and wherever you lodge, I will lodge; your people shall be my people, and your God, my God. Where you die, I will die, and there will I be buried (Ruth 1:16-17).

In fact, Ruth regarded Naomi so highly that she renounced her homeland and voluntarily chose to go to Judah and begin an entirely new life with her mother-in-law. Ruth also admired, respected, and desired the bond her mother-in-law, Naomi, had with the God of Israel.

How high is your respect level for your mother-in-law? A good exercise is to sit down with your spiral notebook or journal and write out "Ten Things I Appreciate About My Mother-in-Law" (or mother...or father...or father-in-law). Believe me, as you focus and dwell on the positive strengths of your husband's mother, you can continually thank God for her qualities and verbalize them to her...and to your husband. This will sweeten your friendship with both!

Ruth was loyal to her mother-in-law—Ruth, as her husband's wife, and Naomi, as Ruth's husband's mother, were family. And, as her fervent declaration reveals, Ruth chose to cleave to Naomi and leave her own pagan homeland. She further pledged undying devotion. To seal her loyalty, Ruth uttered an oath, "The LORD do so to me, and more also, if anything but death parts you and me" (Ruth 1:17).

> *You are on a mission to love, cherish, honor, and respect your family members.*

How can you express your loyalty to your mother-in-law? I would say the Number One way is to say nothing negative about her. Determine that you will not gossip about her. It's easy to fall in line with the "girls" when they start exchanging mother-in-law stories. But, oh no, not you! Why? Because you are a woman and a wife and a daughter-in-law after God's own heart. You are on a mission to love, cherish, honor, and respect your family members. That's God's assignment—and command-ment!—to you.

So when you are tempted to let loose, bite your tongue instead, pray in your heart, and then say nothing. Or you could open your mouth and begin reciting the ten things you most appreciate about your mother-in-law and give testimony to how blessed you are by her. But whatever it takes, please don't get involved in mother-in-law bashing. It poisons your heart, fails to embrace God's perfect plan for your life, hurts her reputation, and leads to no good.

And here's another practice to perfect. Don't put your husband's mother down to him either. Surely the two of you have better, more constructive, more worthy things to talk about than sinking into the shallowness of defaming family members. Instead, burn these instructions from the heart of God into the tablet of yours: "Let no corrupt word proceed out of your mouth, but what is good for necessary edification, that it may impart grace to the hearers." "Let all...evil speaking be put away from you, with all malice" (Ephesians 4:29,31). "Speak evil of no one" (Titus 3:2)... and that includes your in-laws.

Ruth wanted to be with her mother-in-law. Naomi thought first of her two daughters-in-law when she encour-aged them to stay in their familiar homeland. She appealed to each of them, "Go, return to your mother's house. Turn back and go your way" (Ruth 1:8,12). Yet the ever-loyal Ruth followed Naomi down the long road to Bethlehem. Words are one thing, but actions are quite another. Yes,

Ruth pledged her loyalty, and she proceeded to act on her words. Off to Bethlehem she went, walking beside her mother-in-law. Ruth would be a stranger in a strange land, but she wanted to be with Naomi.

I don't know your age, but if you're on the younger end of marriage, express to your mother and mother-in-law your desire to be with them by doing something as simple as extending an invitation to a family dinner at your house or apartment or for a lunch for just the two of you. And if you work, call and say, "Mom (whether she's your mother or mother-in-law), would you like to meet me on my lunch hour? I found this really cute restaurant I think you'd like. I'd love to treat you." Or, "Mom, I'm running out to the mall. Want to go with me? Want to meet me there? I thought we'd have some fun!"

If you're a little older, that means your dear mom or mom-in-law is a little older too. Yes, some things will change...but not your heart. Show your desire to be together by swinging by and picking her up and taking her to the mall or to lunch (or the cafeteria, depending on her age). You can spend time with her by driving her to her hair appointment or doctor's appointment and sitting with her while she waits. And if she's a widow, maybe you can drive her to church or to her family reunion. Or you can send her an airline ticket to come visit you and your bustling family. You can even fix up a room for her...so she can stay as long as she likes.

And how about the far-end of the days of your relationship with parents? I have personally spent parts of about eight years of my life in hospitals and nursing homes because I wanted to be with my parents and parents-in-law as they declined physically and mentally. Being with them meant the expense of airline tickets, being away from my home and immediate family for days at a time, watching their homes while they were being tended to in a care facility.

But here's one scene I'll never forget. As I was walking down the hall in my mother's nursing home on the way to her room, I passed the room of another resident. (By this time, I knew them all.) And there on the bed lay four women—the grandmother who was in her eighties, her daughter in her fifties, and two teenage granddaughters. Honestly, they looked like four girls at a slumber party! They were all laughing and giggling together at something on TV and loving on each other as their arms entwined. The two younger generations of family wanted to be with their senior matriarch. You and I can be sure they—a daughter in the fast-lane of life and two teenagers with all their things to do, people to see, and places to go—gave up something to be in their beloved mother's and grand-mother's dismal room that so needed their cheer. But they did it. And I'm glad they did—and I'm sure they are too, because the next time I walked down that hallway the room was empty. That well-loved mother and grandmother (who was also a mother-in-law to her daughter's husband) had died.

Can't you give up something and spend more time with your parents on both sides soon...before it's too late?

Ruth served her mother-in-law. How? By helping, providing, assisting, and working hard. Life was tough for the two women in the hilly, desert country of Judah. Ruth volunteered to obtain food for Naomi and asked, "Please let me go to the field, and glean heads of grain" (Ruth 2:2). And off she went to literally gather their daily bread...only the barley she reaped was in raw form, which required even more labor from the lovely, servant-hearted Ruth before it could be eaten.

And you? How can you serve the parents in your two families? As surely as the ends of the teeter-totter on a playground exchange positions, so the roles in life reverse. No matter what your parents' ages, health, and stamina are today, one day you will exchange positions just as this poem pictures it.

> As once you stroked my thin and silver hair
> So I stroke yours now at the set of sun.
> I watch your tottering mind, its day's work
>   done,
> As once you watched with forward-looking
>   care
> My tottering feet. I love you as I should.
> Stay with me; lean on me; I'll make no sign.
> I was your child, and now time makes you
>   mine.
> Stay with me yet a while at home, and do me
>   good.[1]

Dear one, ours is a life of service to anybody and everybody. That's what a woman after God's own heart does. And a wife after God's own heart serves her husband first...and then extends that circle of love to include her parents and her in-laws (and even the out-laws!).

Ruth took her mother-in-law's advice. In Ruth we are allowed to behold a truly humble and teachable daughter-in-law. In a very unusual situation, Ruth was counseled by her mother-in-law in the customs of the day in her new land (Ruth 3). And how did Ruth handle being instructed by her mother-in-law? She followed Naomi's counsel to the T...and God worked everything out for Ruth's—and Naomi's—good.

I see just such a heart in my daughter Katherine. Katherine is a member of the MOPS organization (Mothers of Preschoolers), and her mother-in-law, who lives 3,000 miles away, is a mentor in her local MOPS group. I love it when Katherine shares with me the wise advice her mother-in-law has given her regarding parenting and training up her two little ones. Katherine, who is deep into the throes of child-raising, is a sponge. You see, she is not only a woman and a wife after God's own heart, but a mother after His heart as well. And she welcomes every crumb of advice and is a ready listener who takes advice—even from her mother-in-law. As I said, I love this quality in Katherine, and I hope and pray you too, no matter what stage of life you're in, are a wife who seeks, listens to, and follows any godly, practical advice your elders pass on to you. As a proverb warns, "The way of a fool is right in his own eyes, but he who heeds counsel is wise" (Proverbs 12:15).

Ruth blessed her mother-in-law. What a dark and difficult life these two brave and faithful women endured! But, all joy! Ruth married a kinsman...and then a baby was born. And what did Ruth do? She placed her infant son into Naomi's arms. Ruth shared her happiness and her new life as a new family unit with the elderly woman she respected, followed, served, and listened to. And then Ruth went one more step in blessing Naomi...

Ruth let her mother-in-law help her. The Bible paints this tender picture: "Then Naomi took the child and laid him on her bosom, and became a nurse to him" (Ruth 4:16). I wonder if Ruth and Boaz were ever able to pry that baby out of Naomi's arms! But what a sweet scene. A baby *is* new life, but a baby also *brings* new life. And our Naomi enjoyed that blessing of fresh life because a loving, loyal, kind, and giving daughter-in-law let her lend a helping hand. Ruth entrusted her most precious treasure to her mother-in-law. What a daughter-in-law!

Oh my, the lessons are piling up, aren't they? Do you share your little ones with their eager grandparents on both sides? Do you work at finding ways and means of making sure your children are linked to their grandparents? Do you welcome a helping hand, no matter how rusty and out of practice it is?

And then there's the flip side. If you are the grandmother, do you volunteer to help out? Are you communicating your desire to babysit and assist to the busy young mothers in your family? Are you following in dear Naomi's footsteps as she served and eased the load for the younger woman in her life? It saddens me every time a young mom comes up to me at a speaking event and says something like, "I love the way you are involved in your daughters' lives and want to help out with their children. How can I encourage my parents and in-laws to be more involved in our family?"

Dear older reader, your family needs your help, plus I believe it is God's plan. I know distance can be a serious hindrance. But I also believe we grandmothers must pay the price, make the sacrifices, and go the many extra miles—and sometimes hours—required to help out. There are many ways to communicate our heart and our interest. I know I regularly remind my daughters that I want to be their Number One pick for a babysitter at all times. Even if Katherine or Courtney need to go for a haircut, a doctor or dental appointment, a heavy-duty grocery shopping venture, or have a date night, I want to assist them. Plus I want time and input into the hearts and lives of the little ones who make up our next generation.

What can you do today to convey a heart that cares?

"Love Lived Out." I entitled this section with these words for a reason. First, Ruth and Naomi were an "odd couple," but they weren't so oddly matched that love couldn't—and didn't—conquer all. Each woman made the effort, sacrificed, served, honored, respected, and wanted the best for the other. Theirs became a bond that was forever and eternally forged and could not be broken. Each woman lived out God's instructions to "as much as depends on you, live peaceably with all men" (Romans 12:18).

And my second reason for the title "Love Lived Out" is because this noble twosome who traveled together from the mountaintop experiences of bliss into and through a deep and dark valley of sorrow, emerged triumphantly together on the other side. And how did this happen? Each had one person who deeply and genuinely cared for her, albeit an in-law! These ladies put the long line of in-law jokes to rest forever because love lived out formed the strongest bond of all—the bond of family.

Heart Response

Believe me, I have much more I would like to say on this subject of extending love to your family. After all, we didn't even touch upon sibling relationships—both yours and your husband's siblings—and their mates...and the list goes on!

But here's the final challenge to our hearts. If you and your mother or mother-in-law or daughter or daughter-in-law haven't gotten along all that great up to this moment, it's now time for that to change—at least as much as you can make it possible. For now, file away the fact that as a Christian adult married woman—*and* a woman and wife after God's own heart!—you are bigger than the pettiness of bad relationships with your family and in-laws. Indeed, you have all of the resources of a mighty and powerful God at hand to help you. You have the weapon of prayer, and the arsenal of the truths of Scripture, not to mention the sweet strength of God's fruit of the Spirit (Galatians 5:22-23). This means you and I, my beloved reading friend, have no excuses for not bettering our family relationships.

So let's agree to "put away childish things" and ways and "grow up in all things into Him who is the head—Christ" (1 Corinthians 13:11; Ephesians 4:15). That's what a wife after God's own heart does. Now, the question is, Will you? Believe me, doing so will *really* make a difference in your marriage!

Little Things That Make a Big Difference

1. Say *yes* as often as you can.

When it comes to getting together, babysitting for one another, car-pooling, housesitting, or helping out extended family members, say *yes* as often as you can. You are a *family*, for goodness' sake! Therefore you should also be a *team*. Each good deed done is a link in the chain that will draw you closer to one another until your hearts are knit together.

2. Budget for family get-togethers.

I'm sure you've heard people explain that they can't go to their family reunion because they don't have the money...yet they continue to drive through fast-food restaurants, eat out, purchase large-screen TVs, subscribe to cable and internet lines, and on and on their list of optional monetary outlay goes. If something is important to us, we always seem to make a way for it. And family should be important—important enough to make some sacrifices, both financially and time-wise. So budget (see Chapter 5) in a way that "buys" you time to be with your extended family. The Law of Good Relationships says, "The more time you spend together, the better friends you become."

3. Visit your parents.

Certainly there is some leaving and cleaving that must take place when you marry (see Chapter 2), but you are also to honor your parents. A key way to show your love and appreciation is to visit them and to invite them to visit you. Yes, it requires some planning, work, time, and expense on your part. But the dividends will begin to build and build until you have a wonderful relationship. So take calendar in hand and call and invite each set of parents for a visit. When is the best time for them to come? For you to go visit them? Will the dates work out for everyone? Stay at it until you have a working plan. And don't rule out meeting halfway for a weekend together. Whatever it takes in time and money, give it your best effort. You'll be glad you did as the years roll by and the good memories pile up!

4. Stay in touch.

You're a master planner when it comes to your home, husband, and children. So put that brain of yours to work on figuring out as many ways as you can for staying in touch with both sets of parents and all siblings, nieces, and nephews. After all, they are *yours,* given to you by God. Therefore you have a God-ordained role in their lives, and they in yours as well. So use that cell phone with so many monthly minutes and call your family often. Put that internet cable you are paying for to work on your family and email away. Send pictures, photographs, updates, round-robin newsletters. Share funny stories, ball scores, prayer requests...whatever it takes to stay in touch.

5. Take lots of pictures.

I'm sorry, but I can't resist this one. It seems obvious, and yet it's so easy to let family times together just happen without a record of them. So carry a small camera with you or pick up a disposable one, especially when you know you are going to be with family. Ask a stranger to snap a quick picture of you with your relatives. Get a shot of your parents hugging and smiling. The same with you and your siblings. Line up the nieces and nephews and fire away! Don't let a single get-together slip by unrecorded.

6. Pray for your family.

You cannot neglect the person you are praying for, and you cannot hate the person you are praying for. So as a wife after God's own heart, make it your heart's goal to pray faithfully for *all* family members—both the in-laws and the out-laws! Create a prayer page for each person. Then begin noting birthdates, anniversaries, favorite foods and colors, hobbies and collections. Companies and corporations go to great lengths to find out and update all kinds of information about their customers and account holders. Surely you can do the same for family!

9

Tending Your Career

Women must likewise be...faithful in all things.
1 TIMOTHY 3:11 NASB

What is a woman after God's own heart? She is a woman who, like King David of old, seeks with all her heart to fulfill God's will (Acts 13:22). And that, my friend and fellow seeker of God's heart, is what we are pursuing in this book about our "career" as a wife after God's own heart—to *learn* what God's will is so that we can *do* God's will, for as someone noted, "To know God's will is man's greatest treasure; to do His will is life's greatest privilege."[1]

Doing God's Will

Before we tackle the topic of tending to a job, I want to remind you that throughout this book we've been discovering what God's will is for a woman and a wife. Here's what we've established to be our God-given priorities so far.

Love God—A wife after God's own heart is first and foremost a woman whose heart belongs to God. God is not only her first priority, He is her ultimate priority and her consuming passion. As a Christian she makes and takes the time to nurture her relationship with God. She has no greater love than her love for God and His Son, Jesus Christ. She delights in keeping God's "first and great commandment"—"You shall love the LORD your God with all your heart, with all your soul, and with all your mind" (Matthew 22:37-38). This passionate and passionately tended love-relationship with the Lord creates a rich, deep reservoir she can draw from in order to whole-heartedly tend to her other God-given roles and relationships.

Love her husband—As a wife, a married woman practices God's priorities by loving her husband (Titus 2:4). After God, she gives her all to her mate-for-life. She makes and takes the time to achieve a best-friend relationship with him. After her time with God, she pours out the best portions of her time, energy, love, and devotion to build and better her marriage. She focuses her efforts on her marriage and on her marriage partner—on improving his life, on serving him, and on striving to live together in harmony. She seeks, with God's help, to live out her God-given roles as a wife—to help, follow, respect, and love her husband.

Love her children—As a mother and as someone who desires to do God's will, God's woman will next make and take the time required to cultivate relationships with her children, no matter what their ages (Titus 2:4). Hers is a lifelong commitment to be an involved, hands-on, fiercely loving and caring mother. She is going to raise her children and give them their primary input. That's her role...and another one of her passions. Why, she's a mother after God's own heart!

Love her home—To a wife after God's own heart, home is next (Titus 2:5). She directs her energies toward building, watching over, and establishing a place where the successful nurturing of her marriage and family can take place. She loves her home (and her family!), takes joy in being there, improves it with her efforts, and is "the queen of fuss" when it comes to her home-sweet-home! She lovingly fusses over the people...and the place.

Commenting on the woman who concentrates on living out these first four God-given priorities, one has noted, "The woman who creates and sustains a home, and under whose hands children grow up to be strong and pure men and women is a creator second only to God."[2]

Love and serve God's people—A woman who aspires to wear the label "a woman after God's own heart" and to possess such a heart has a vital relationship with Jesus Christ. And that relationship thrusts her into the family of God, the body of Christ—the church. As a Christian she is spiritually gifted by God "for the profit of all" (1 Corinthians 12:7), to benefit the church universal and, in particular, the church where she attends. This service to God and His people is a duty and a responsibility every Christian is given, and it is also a privilege that cannot be bought. This service is not optional.

But oh, the blessings that belong to the woman who follows God's plan for serving others! We'll spend an entire chapter on these blessings later, but for now, mark it well—our service to God's people in the church is highly important. It is assigned by God and therefore comes *before* and ranks *higher* in priority than a job, career, or profession.

Now, with our God-given priorities in mind, we can ask and answer a few questions.

Asking...and Answering a Few Questions

I know that many women work. In fact, I think the latest statistic is that more than 50 percent of married women are in the workforce. I'm a realist, and I'm in touch with thousands of women on a regular basis. I receive a lot of mail and email, talk personally with busy working women at conferences, and repeatedly participate in question-and-answer sessions. From personal experience I know about the hearts and lives of God's women, and I want to give you some food for thought, some prompts for heart-evaluation, and some checkpoints to pray about.

Two letters in particular seemed to go straight to the heart of the matter. In one a precious woman asked, "How does a woman with a 9 A.M. to 5 P.M. job keep her priorities in order?" Another sister-in-Christ wrote, "What advice do you have for someone who has to go to a job, then come home and do cleaning, cooking, discipline the children, etc.?"

Obviously these are complicated questions, and each woman asked hers from a different set of circumstances, painstakingly taking pages to lay out the details of the conditions of her life. How did I answer these letters? And how can you apply these truths to your own situation? Please take the time to answer this set of questions. Doing so will help you to understand and evaluate your own situation.

1. *Why am I working?* Asking yourself this question is like taking a good look in the mirror. There are women whose husbands want them to work, and there are those who are working because they want to. I've even talked to women whose husbands don't want them to work, yet they continue to keep their jobs. Your answer to this question will help clarify your motives and reasons for having a job.

2. *Have I explained my desires and concerns to my husband?* If you fall into the category of working because your husband insists or wants you to work, then you need to pray diligently and ask God for wisdom in approaching your husband (see #9). You need to sweetly and intelligently (versus emotionally) present your case and sound reasons for staying at home to your husband. Use all of your good communication skills (see Chapter 3). Put them to work for you as you discuss priorities. And be sure you follow Esther's example in Esther 5—*wait* until the right time to present your case!

3. *Have I properly researched my options?* Is there a way I can stay at home and still bring in an income? Could I manage a business from home? Could I make boutique items to sell? Is there a small internet business I could initiate? Perhaps I can get a newspaper route? (I know at least a dozen women who throw papers in the early morning while listening to Bible teachings on tape, memorizing Scripture, and praying for their families.) Or will my employer allow me to do my work at home? (So many of my readers are discovering this is an option that is getting *yes* as an answer!)

What about saving more and spending less? How much money could I save by cooking instead of eating out? Can I join a food co-op to save money? Do I really need the new clothes? Do the kids have to have the latest toys? Can we make do with the tools we have on hand?

I have treated this subject of options to a full-time job at great length in my book *Beautiful in God's Eyes—The Treasures of the Proverbs 31 Woman.*[3] That book centers around the context of the life of the remarkable woman portrayed in Proverbs, Chapter 31. "The Proverbs 31 woman," as she is referred to, crafted a life of skillfully managed priorities, industry, and productivity. Drawing from her daily life, I worked hard to give biblical and practical advice to women like you, whether you are a woman who wants to stay at home or a woman who works outside the home. I do not hesitate to direct you to this book for a fuller picture of this most excellent model for every woman and wife after God's own heart.

4. *Do I have goals that will allow me to quit working?* Goals such as paying off debts, stepping down from full-time work to part-time work, selling items not needed, a strict (or stricter!) budget, downsizing expenses? Rather than thinking that staying at home is not an option, you and your husband can make quitting your job a goal. Once it's a goal, you can take the intermediary steps that will one day make your dream a reality.

5. *What can (or must) be eliminated from my life?* If your husband insists that you work, streamlining your life is mandatory. You'll have to carefully curb your outings, commitments, participation, and involvements (even in worthy purposes and pursuits) that can cut into managing your home life and nurturing fulfilling relationships there.

> *As a working woman you will have to truly believe and live like every minute counts—and it does!*

6. *How can I do a better job of managing my time?* This is a question each woman should ask every day. But for the working woman, it is a must! To make the machinery of a quality life run smoothly, you'll need to master and become an expert at time management. Read every book you can on the subject. Take every shortcut you can. Learn the tricks of doing more in less time...and of working smarter instead of harder. As a working woman you will have to truly believe and live like every minute counts—and it does!

7. *Am I neglecting my relationship with the Lord?* Again, if you work, your time with the Lord will energize all that you must do. So make sure you spend quality time with Him in prayer and study. It will make you sweeter, more patient, and boost your love for the family you are to serve each day when you return home.

8. *Is my perspective right?* If you work, your attitude should be that your job is "simply something else I do." It is not your life. Yes, it takes a lot of time, but no, it is not your priority mission in life. Your real, God-given assignments are waiting for you at home. True fulfillment comes from the strong and lasting relationships you are building right under your own roof. Family lasts a lifetime—a job does not.

9. *Am I diligently and fervently praying for God to work in my husband's heart?* Do you believe that God hears and answers prayer, my friend? Ask *Him* to move in your husband's heart. Also ask God to reveal solutions and ideas that will provide the means for you to stay at home. And ask Him for His grace to sustain your many responsibilities.

10. *Am I faithfully endeavoring to follow God's priorities for my life?* Every woman and wife after God's own heart must acknowledge that no job and no set of circumstances can ever negate God's Word to us as married women to love Him, love our husbands, love our children, love our homes, and love and serve His people. It is imperative that we follow God's guidelines in these vital areas.

A Word of Testimony

I grew up in a wonderful, busy, bustling family where every one of the children began working at an early age. That meant that I began my working "career" by tending to our neighbors' houses and pets while they were on vacation. Next came babysitting in the neighborhood. Then at age 16 I got my first after-school job at a local hardware store helping the bookkeeper post the day's sales receipts. And at Christmastime I always had an additional gift-wrapping job. My summers were also filled with jobs as my parents and I were saving for my college fund. On and on my little résumé of part-time and odd jobs went. Even when I finally went off to college, I worked after school, on weekends, and during the summers.

Then I met Jim. And guess what? Jim had grown up in exactly the same way. Jim had begun his long list of work experiences at age 14 by pitching watermelons off a truck at his local grocery store. So the two of us workhorses married and kept right on working while we completed our college educations. And we did it! We finished college, graduating on the same day. I wish you could see the one-and-only picture we have of that day. We are standing together, diplomas in hand, with black circles under our eyes, haggard looking...wearing the two biggest smiles you ever saw. Yes, we did it!

By then Jim and I had been married one whole year. Wow, what a year! And then we set off on the trail of wherever Jim's career as a pharmacist and a pharmaceutical salesman took us. Wherever that was, I continued to work.

For a few months, I logged well production for an oil company. Then I taught in a rural school for nine months. During this time Jim and I were able to use our earnings and savings to purchase our first little home. Then another transfer came...and I worked in an insurance company keeping track of group insurance payments. Then another transfer came...and I ended up being the executive secretary to an educator who ran an intellectual retreat center.

But I have to tell you this. Throughout all of the going to college, the working here and there, and the transfers and moves, I knew that the day our first baby arrived my working would be over. And sure enough, the day baby Katherine arrived, I was done being a "career" woman. And 13 months later, Katherine was joined by her sister, Courtney.

Have I held down a job since then? I have to say *yes*. Exactly twice, to be exact. The first was when both of my daughters were in grade school. I taught in the preschool, two mornings a week, for nine months, in exchange for half-tuition for Katherine and Courtney. And the second time was many years later when our daughters entered high school, were in braces, driving....Well, you know the scene—and the expenses! During this short stint I did bookkeeping two nights a week in my home. After the girls were in bed, I pulled out our card table, set up the tub

> *Your home—
> the people and
> the place—is
> always to be
> the priority
> over any
> profession.*

of records that had been dropped off, turned on some music, put in a few hours' work, and then set the tub by the door, ready to be picked up the next day.

So, yes, I worked for those two periods of time that were carefully arranged around our family schedule. But the goal was that no one (husband, children, home, or ministry) would suffer and (hopefully!) everyone would benefit.

I have to say that I am a homebody. Why? Because that's where my husband is, where my children were in days gone by, where my home is, and where the preparations required to teach God's Word to the women in my church (a part of my service to God's people) took place for so many years. Because that's where my heart is, was, and ever will be. Therefore I try to do everything at home and from home. Now, for instance, I write at home. And if I travel to speak, Jim and I go together. And if he travels to speak, I accompany him, if at all possible.

But I don't write or teach at the expense of my marriage, family, and home. No, I seek daily to fuel my relationship with God, with Jim, with my married children and grandchildren, to love, care for, and fuss over our home, and to serve the body of Christ through my writing and speaking ministry. I do laundry, make meals, keep house, run errands...and *then* write. My eye is on my home, my heart is at home, and my deepest desire is to live out the priorities God has set down for me as a married woman (...which also means that my deepest fear is that I will fail to do so).

So I ask you, as I ask myself regularly, Where is your heart? Is it at home—at your home-sweet-home? Every woman, and perhaps especially the woman who tends a career, must ask and answer that question every day. You see, being a woman and a wife after God's own heart is all about the heart—your heart.

Heart Response

I know every married woman's situation is different. Many work outside the home, and many don't. But every married woman is called to practice her priorities, which as a woman after God's own heart are God's priorities. Therefore you and I must ever and always remember this—No price can be put on doing God's will. No paycheck or dollar amount of income and benefits from a job can ever substitute for living your life according to God's will. Your job from God is to help your husband, to nurture your relationship with him, to love and care for your children, and to be about the business of building your house. You may have a job, but your home—the people and the place—is always to be the priority over any profession.

Beloved, we've been considering a woman's priorities in this chapter and in this book. We've been searching for help with what God wants for us as wives. The priorities we've uncovered to this point are revealed in the Bible and are unchanging. They come to us from and as "the word of God which lives and abides forever" (1 Peter 1:23). "The counsel of the LORD stands forever, the plans of His heart to all generations" (Psalm 33:11). That means that no matter what we want, or what society tells us to want, or what anyone else wants for us, we as women after God's own heart are to want what God wants. We may tend a career, but we must first and foremost desire to fulfill God's will when it comes to the priorities He wisely and sovereignly sets down for our lives.

Where is your heart?

(And P.S., if you are having trouble accepting, desiring, and owning God's will for your life as a married woman, then "ask God to make you willing to be willing"![4])

Little Things That Make a Big Difference

1. Review your priorities every day.

As a Christian, everything you do is to be done excellently...and that includes your job. Part of what this means is that you must constantly check your priorities. Reviewing them first thing every morning helps you keep your marriage, family, home, and job in perspective. It helps you remember that your marriage, family, and home are more important in God's big picture than your job. It helps you remember that as a Christian wife it is the time you spend with your husband at home *before* and *after* work that is your greatest and grandest work for the day!

Be careful not to view your job as more important than the work you do at home—building lasting relationships and creating a home that blesses you and your family. Those at home will never be impressed by the work they never see you do on a job, but they will carry forever in their hearts the memories of a loving, attentive mom and the knowledge that they were Number One!

2. Aim for an organized morning.

If the time you spend at home with your husband is priority time, then aim for an organized morning that allows you and your sweetie time to talk, touch base, have some breakfast, and a word of prayer. If you have time to clean up the kitchen too, you'll be extremely glad later. If you're also trying to get children off to school, then they also need time to talk, touch base, have breakfast, and share a word of prayer. So put the skills you use at work to work for you at home. Do some micro-managing—do some detailed planning.

What can and must you do the night before so everyone isn't yelling at each other the next morning, when they're running late and frustrated because they can't find what they need? Can you set the breakfast table the night before? Can you set out the cereal boxes, vitamins, and sugar? And don't forget the devotional book and Bible! Put school books, backpacks, and briefcases by the front door. Lay out car keys, cell phones, purses, and wallets. If anyone takes a lunch, fix as much as you can after dinner and set it out on the kitchen counter. Run the dishwasher, take out the trash, and, of course, get a good night's sleep. *Whew!* Know in your heart that everything you do the night before pays huge dividends the next morning!

3. Use your lunch hour wisely.

If you work an eight-hour day, those eight hours belong to your employer. However, your lunch hour belongs to you. And if you treat it well and use it wisely, it can become one of your greatest opportunities for staying on top of things or even getting ahead at home.

What can you do on a lunch hour? Pay the bills. Run some errands. Pick up food items and dry cleaning. Make important personal phone calls. Get your hair cut. Work on a continuing education certificate. Write letters. Do your Bible-study homework. Have a doctor or dental appointment. Some women even fit in a workout on their lunch hour. See how many things you can do in the five lunch hours that are yours during the week so your evenings and weekends can be memorable family times.

4. Be all there when you are at home.

Ah, home-sweet-home! At last your day at work is over. And now your "job" is to be sure it's over. Leave work at work! Leave the disputes, emotions, confusion, and any hurt feelings or disappointments you may have experienced on the job at the job. Your husband deserves your attention when he gets home. *He* is the most important person in your life. He deserves a listening ear, a nice meal, and a pleasant evening.

So train yourself to be all there when you are at home. Pray on the way home. Thank God that your day at work is O-V-E-R! Purpose not to rehash your day and the latest office gossip. You are a wife (and a mom and a homemaker) first...and then a worker. So, once again, when you finally make it home, be all there! Give your all. Enjoy your family to the max. Soak up every pleasure home and family bring to your heart. Ah, home-sweet-home!

10

Making Time for Fun

> *Rise up, my love, my fair one,*
> *and come away!*
> SONG OF SOLOMON 2:13

As you now know from the previous chapter, both Jim and I are workhorses. And that's a good thing! Being hard workers means that we each strive to be conscientious, faithful, and disciplined. But there's a downside to such dedication. Can you guess what it is? Well, let me fill in the blank for you. It's failing to stop and make time for fun as a couple. If Jim and I aren't careful, we can give ourselves to all work and no play! So, just as we learned to persevere at our work and in the upkeep of our home, we have learned (and are still learning!) to remember to have some fun along the way.

How Did It All Begin?

When I met my dear Jim, the nickname given to him by his friends in college was "Smilin' Jim George." He had bright eyes, a huge smile, a quick laugh, and a light-hearted, adventuresome attitude toward life. What fun we had as we began spending time together! Sure, much of our time was filled with studying in the library and typing our papers and reports. But we also enjoyed seeing the "Boomer Sooners" play live at the University of Oklahoma (our alma mater) on Saturday afternoons, being with Jim's or my friends, going bowling or on frequent Coke dates, and then talking on the phone for hours afterward. There was never a dull moment, and fun was at the center of all we did. We made everything fun—even poring over our studies and being responsible employees.

After "Smilin' Jim" and I married, the fun escalated. Marriage meant we could take off on weekend adventures to go water skiing, to play at the Six Flags amusement park, to stay a night in Oklahoma City when Jim went to his Army Reserve meetings. As a couple we tried snow skiing, sailing, and tennis. We took night classes together at the local community college where we learned the basics of photography and how to play chess. We learned how to strip and refinish old furniture to furnish our little apartment, even completing a class project on designing and building bookcases...and the list goes on. Again, there was never a dull moment.

This is how our wonderful friendship and marriage all began. And it's been a refreshing exercise for me to go back and revisit the "fun" memories of the good times we had. And now I want to ask you to do the same thing. Just take a few minutes to remember—to really remember!—how it all began for you and your husband. I guarantee that recalling the memories of the playful pleasures you once enjoyed will be the spark that ignites more fun in your day today! Your bond with your husband probably began the same way mine did with Jim—with the craziness and fun shared by two people hopelessly and helplessly in love. The two of you, too, probably talked your heads and ears off. And you, too, were probably both deliriously happy.

But...What Happened to the Fun?

If you're like most couples, real life set in all too soon. After your honeymoon was over, reality began to nibble away at the fun that was unique to the two of you. On the heels of all of the thrills came such challenges as job pressures, monthly income and bill paying, learning to communicate (with a few disagreements thrown in along the way!), dealing with family...well, you know the scene! Here are a few of the culprits that showed up on Jim's and my doorstep. See if you can relate.

Responsibility—There's no doubt that the seriousness of life can cut its way into your fun as a couple. It's a fact that the older we get the more serious life becomes. And it's sobering to have to "grow up," to mature, to put away childish things (1 Corinthians 13:11), to shoulder greater and greater responsibility. As Christians we have a purpose for our life and work to do for Christ (2 Timothy 1:9). We are also to be diligent and faithful in all things (1 Timothy 3:11). Properly honoring and representing Christ calls for us to put away procrastination, sloppiness, and negligence (Titus 2:5). We are also to do all things "heartily, as to the Lord" (Colossians 3:23) and to "serve the Lord Christ" in all we do (verse 24). These real responsibilities of daily life are definitely serious...and challenging.

Money matters—Every couple has to not only make money but also make ends meet. On top of taking care of your relationship with God and your husband and your workmanship at home, you now have the added pressure of money. Almost 100 percent of newlyweds have more month than money! And that spells *pressure!* When things are stressed in the Money Department, things can be stressed in the Marriage Department, which can also affect the Fun Department. We can soon wonder, "What happened to the fun? Is this all there is to married life?"

Children—No parent would argue against the biblical truth that babies are a blessing. "Behold, children are a heritage from the LORD" and "happy is the man who has his quiver full of them" (Psalm 127:3,5). A blessing, yes! But children can stretch you to the limit. They arrive with a long list of added responsibilities on the parents' parts, which means there is more growing up to do, more maturing that must take place as you begin to care for a completely helpless human being. Which soon leads to...

Exhaustion—If you and your honey are like Jim and me, you get up early and stay up late. You're just trying to take care of the business and responsibilities of life, not to mention the number of children being added to your two-some! And soon both husband and wife are exhausted (which means "to be used up and completely expended, drained of power and tired out")...and *that's* no fun!

And now another fact must be faced: No matter what your age or how long you've been married, there is a lot for a wife, mother, and homemaker after God's own heart to do! And honestly, I haven't seen the number or the intensity of my list of obligations go down as my age has gone up. No, it's quite the opposite. As soon as our child-raising years were over and our daughters married, Jim and I were faced with the decline and deaths of all our parents. While responsibilities diminished on the parental end of our life, they boomed, exploded, and multiplied on the other end with the addition of two sons-in-law and five new babies for our family! Oh no, things have *not ever* slowed down for us! No wonder on some days we both wonder, "But what happened to the wonderful fun things we used to do?"

Discouragement—Every day has its joy (Psalm 118:24). And each new sunrise is a vision of hope (Psalm 30:5). But each day also comes with its trials (James 1:2). When you add up responsibility, children, exhaustion, and mix in a few failures along the way in any or all of these departments, it's easy to become discouraged. If a woman and wife isn't careful how she handles such discouragement, she can become depressed. Whenever I speak on my book *Loving God with All Your Mind*[1] (which contains the story of my difficulties with depression and the truths from

Scripture that continue to give me daily victory), I share these startling statistics:

- Some form of depression affects over 17.5 million Americans each year.

- The highest overall age for depression is between 25 and 44.

- Depression can affect anyone, regardless of background, though major depression strikes women twice as often as men.[2]

And what are a handful of the culprits that can lead to depression? "Unhappily married people have the highest rates" of depression. Plus "loss of jobs and major financial reverses" many times contribute to depression. (Are you noticing the many topics already covered in this book about nurturing a marriage after God's own heart?) And every woman knows that "down-type feelings" and "feelings of sadness"[3] can easily lead to depressed moods that sap her and her marriage of not only fun, but of God-given joy.

Recapturing the Fun

So what can you (and I!) as a wife do to curb such joy-robbers? What can you do to help recapture the fun in your marriage? What can you do to weave the laughter, the impish gaiety, the sparkle back into the climate in your home and your heart?

First of all, realize that joy must begin in *your heart*. The Bible explains that "a merry heart makes a cheerful

countenance" (Proverbs 15:13).
In other words, your thoughts
and attitudes—not your circumstances—make all the
difference. So what are you
thinking? Are you fueling
memories of past events that
are creating a cesspool of bitterness or disappointment?
Are you kindling a critical
spirit? A sad spirit? As one

> *If you belong to God through His Son Jesus Christ, yours is the deepest, purist, fullest joy that any person can possess.*

scholar comments regarding this verse, "Sad thoughts crush the spirit,"[4] So you and I must cultivate such a merry heart...and that begins with a head full of happy thoughts and a heart full of happy attitudes. As the same writer put it, "Gay heart, gay looks."

Next, realize that the ultimate source of all joy is *the Lord!* "The *joy* of the LORD is your strength" (Nehemiah 8:10). Everyone (including you) who trusts in the Lord and takes refuge in Him can and should *rejoice* (Psalm 5:11)! And "the fruit of the Spirit is...*joy*" (Galatians 5:22). Dear wife, if you belong to God through His Son Jesus Christ, yours is the deepest, purest, fullest joy that any person can possess. So...

🐝 Purposefully rejoice each day—The psalmist exulted, "This is the day the LORD has made; we *will* rejoice and be glad in it" (Psalm 118:24). Before your feet hit the floor each morning (and before you speak to your husband), remind your heart and soul of this truth. And remind yourself again every time you hit a speed bump during your God-designed day. Purposefully rejoice.

🎵 Purposefully play music—I play music practically all day every day. After years of discouragement and depression, I *learned* to get the music going early each day…which gets the music going in my heart! King David, "the sweet psalmist of Israel" (2 Samuel 23:1), knew well that music lifts the soul and turns a person's thoughts and emotions toward God when he organized music as a part of the temple worship services (1 Chronicles 25). Music will set your spirit free from this disheartening world to soar and sing. "Psalms and hymns and spiritual songs" will cause *you* to sing and make melody in *your* heart to the Lord (Ephesians 5:19).

🎵 Purposefully put on a smile—Go ahead, do it! Then share it. Give it away! Let the joy within your heart rejoice the hearts of others …beginning with the one closest to you, the one who would benefit the most— your precious husband. The Bible explains that "a merry heart makes a cheerful countenance" and "the light of

> *Let the joy within your heart rejoice the hearts of others…beginning with the one closest to you… your precious husband!*

the eyes rejoices the heart" (Proverbs 15:13,30). Your cheerful countenance and smile will have a heartwarming effect on those in your presence. It's contagious! It gladdens the heart of everyone you meet. What a gift!

Please realize that *your creativity* is a key to opening the door of the Fun Department. Many wives wait for their husbands to initiate the fun. A wife may dream of a husband who sits around "dreaming up" creative and romantic events and outings (as if he isn't busy enough providing for the family, taking care of the finances and the upkeep of the home and car, being a good dad after he gets home from work...and on and on his list goes!). I had my wake-up call in this area when I was a seminary wife...who was sitting around waiting for my poor Jim, a full-time student with four part-time jobs, to "dream up" a little fun for the two of us. A guest speaker encouraged all of us wives to become "the planner of fun" for our marriage. He said, "You plan and prepare the picnic or whatever. I guarantee, your husband will show up and he will enjoy it. But don't wait for him to think of it!" So be creative! What will you plan first?

Where Do I Start?

I'll share a lot of "Little Things That Make a Big Difference" in the Fun Department in your marriage in a few pages, but for now here are a few "little things" some of our couple-friends do for fun.

Cook together—One thing my daughter Katherine and her Paul enjoy doing for fun is to pick a dish they would like to eat. It has to be something new and different. Then they go on-line together and find a recipe on the internet, print it out, make their grocery list of ingredients, shop for the items together, divide up the labor—the washing, chopping, measuring, mixing, stirring—get in the kitchen together, and *voila!* a mouth-watering and fun memory! Not only do they have fun, but, as you well know, they have to develop some pretty good communication skills to both work in the kitchen on a mutual project. And now Paul and Katherine extend their gift to others. Every time they come visit Jim and me, they find or bring a recipe, go to our local grocery store, take over the kitchen, and treat us to a special, fun meal!

Play a game together—This sounds trite and is probably on everyone's list of ways to have fun, but few couples will actually give up their TV time to do it. The specific couple I'm thinking of was staying in a hotel in Hawaii where Jim and I were speaking. We continually saw this laughing twosome sitting on their lanai, playing games like chess and cribbage. They had clearly turned their backs on their in-room television viewing and movies to play games and have some fun. Both Jim and I commented on the two of them and the fun they were obviously having. And both Jim and I said, "Why don't more couples do that?! Why spend money going out when something this much fun is free?"

Tour a museum together—Jim and I have best friends who, for 20 years, have toured a museum exhibit once a month. Together they watch the newspapers for listings of exhibits in nearby museums. Then they get their calendars out and "make a date." Like two little children, they anticipate their outing. Then the day finally arrives...and the fun begins! They plan to have fun, make time for fun, have fun, and have a string of fun memories. And can you imagine the fun Jim and I have had over the years listening to them talk about what they've seen and learned on their exploits? Why, they've even included the two of us on a few of their museum outings. What fun...and for little or no money!

Go downtown together—My pastor and his wife know how to have fun on their day off. They take a ferry ride from the Olympic Peninsula side of Puget Sound here in Washington and spend a part of the day in downtown Seattle. They go everywhere on foot, even in the rain. Nothing stops them! They know every little coffee shop, sandwich bar, farmers market, tourist attraction, trolley route, side street, and back alley. And they stay physically fit from pounding the pavement on Seattle's steep hills. It's their "thing," the little inexpensive, adventuresome thing they do that is just theirs to enjoy. I'm sure that looking forward to their thing and their day is something they savor all week long. Now, where is "downtown" for you? And how long has it been since you've been there?

Go to a park together—Let me point again to our Paul and Katherine. Paul never goes anywhere without a ball or a frisbee. And that includes going to his present job on Madison Avenue in New York City. On many of Paul's lunch breaks or after work, Katherine will bundle up the babies and either walk, take a train, or a taxi to meet him. And off they go to The Park—as in Central Park—to talk as they push the stroller so their toddlers can run and play, to toss a frisbee or a ball, and to stay late and catch fireflies. Every city park is special...and free! Now, when can you and your honey go there together?

Heart Response

For years I've approached my daily planner every morning with what I call "The Three F's" in mind. These "F's" represent major areas of my life that I need to tend to each day in addition to a few of the obvious ones—my spiritual life and my relationship with Jim. They are Family, Fitness, and Finishing Fully (as in finishing my writing, my speech-writing, my projects, whatever it is that needs to be done—and finished!—each particular day).

Well, one morning my darling Jim took his pen in hand and reached over and wrote in a fourth "F" that he wanted me to add to my daily aims—*Fun!* I hadn't realized it, but the culprits to fun had eaten their way into that important element upon which Jim's and my relationship had begun!

And so now, after 38 years of marriage, I am paying more attention to fun.

I opened this chapter with one of my favorite "couple" verses in the Bible. The words are those remembered by a bride, the Shulamite. They are the prose "voiced" (Song of Solomon 2:8) by her bridegroom to and for her, his "beloved." In her dream or her reflections, her husband cries out to her to "rise up, my love, my fair one, and come away!" (verse 13).

Is it possible that you, dear wife, need to lighten up? To have some fun? To be more playful? To get out there and do something enjoyable with your husband? The married couple described in Song of Solomon were madly and passionately in love. And it was of her husband, the person she walked and visited and played with and had fun with, that this wife said, "This is my beloved, and this is my friend" (Song of Solomon 5:16).

How's your friendship with your beloved? Are you purposefully, willfully, and decisively making time for fun?

Little Things That Make a Big Difference

1. Plan one fun activity a week.

Someone needs to be in charge of the Fun Department, and maybe that someone can be you! Begin your stint as the chief organizer of your fun-as-a-couple time by planning one activity per week. It doesn't have to cost a lot—or even cost anything. All you have to do is be creative.

Can you get into the kitchen and cook a meal together? How about setting up the fondue pot and cooking while you eat? Can you go bike riding for a few hours with a picnic in your backpacks? Or what about getting up before daylight on a Saturday for a walk on the beach and gathering seashells while the sun is rising? Could you have a "backward" meal—begin with dessert and end with salad—or have your husband draw numbers that you've assigned to items on your dinner menu, and eat them in the order he picks?

See how many things you can come up with for fun that costs little or nothing. Keep a list going so you never lose a great idea for fun. And sure, once in a while do something fun that costs a little—something you've saved up for. What a bountiful treasure of wonderful memories you will be creating!

2. Recreate an old date from the past.

Think of something you and your husband both enjoyed in the past and then try to recreate it. How about attending a college football game? Or visiting a favorite restaurant from the past—whether it's a fancy place, a dive, or a greasy spoon? Whatever it is, it's a part of your past. So revisit it and keep the memory alive. Did you spend time together in days gone by bowling? Playing miniature golf? Roller skating? Camping? Then do it again. Let the good old days roll again!

3. Recreate your honeymoon.

Maybe you will and maybe you won't be able to actually recreate your honeymoon. Many couples do. But you can definitely pull out your wedding photos or pop in your wedding video. You can purchase the smallest of small bakery cakes and concoct some kind of punch and serve it with a handful of mixed nuts and butter mints. Just have fun!

4. Make each anniversary unique.

Each anniversary is a milestone. That's one more year of being together that you and your hubby can celebrate! Don't wait for your busy husband to come up with a plan for this unique day. Make this a special and fun day. Give the children an early dinner and an early bedtime, and then have a special meal for just the two of you. And then plan for a special time of intimacy.

And here's another factor. Very few couples can actually celebrate their anniversary on the actual date. Decide that that's okay. It's not the date that's important—it's the celebration of another year of marriage that is. So work around commitments and responsibilities and family obligations. Just be sure you celebrate somehow and in some way.

5. Choose a couple hobby.

I'm sure you can think of a multitude of potential couple hobbies—golf, tennis, biking, camping, kayaking, chess, refinishing furniture, and photography are some examples. You name it! Your "little thing" assignment is to experiment and choose what you would like to be yours as a couple. Find a hobby that you both can participate in and enjoy with a minimal amount of training. Remember, some hobbies become more enjoyable as you get better at them or take a few classes together. But also remember, these are "little things," so find something that only takes a little something to get you started. Then be sure you schedule it into your lives.

6. Make a list of things you've always wanted to do.

What have either of you always wanted to do that can be done together? Pick one. Was it your idea?

Then you are in charge of making it happen. Visit that old, musty, used bookstore downtown that has always intrigued you. Then enjoy a cup of coffee or hot cocoa next door at the coffee shop. Take a picnic to a city park. (Now, why is it you haven't ever been there before?) These are little things... and there should be a ton of little things on your list. But you can also put some big things on it too, such as having someone take a picture of the two of you at the top of the Eiffel Tower, touring Israel, walking on the Great Wall of China, going on a photo safari in Africa. Wow, what fun the two of you will have making your list—a list that spans the globe and unites your hearts...even if you never actually do most of the things on it!

11

Serving the Lord

For you serve the Lord Christ.
COLOSSIANS 3:24

Some acts are life-changing. We don't know their impact at the time, but afterward our days are never the same. This is exactly what happened to me one quiet Sunday afternoon. Our two little preschoolers were napping. Church had been thrilling that morning. And Jim and I sat down to go through an exercise together—and it set off a bomb in our lives as Christians and established the direction we have followed for the past 30 years. The two of us—as a couple—asked our hearts one question, which we tried to answer on paper: "What are your lifetime goals?"

How did my list turn out? Well, believe me, I still have the original papers! With a heart filled with passion for God and thanksgiving to my Savior, I targeted these three desires:

1. To be a growing woman of God.

2. To be a supportive and encouraging wife and mother.

3. To teach the Bible so that women's lives are changed.

So far in our book about being a wife after God's own heart, we have focused on growing in the Lord and being a supportive and encouraging wife and mother. Now it's time to address our responsibility and duty as Christian women to serve the Lord.

Serving as a Christian

Every Christian, married or not, is to serve the Lord and the church, the body of Christ. Like the old-time saying reminds us, "We are saved to serve, not to be served." Several factors help us to live a life of service.

We serve out of motivation—Here's a truth about every believer: Before we become Christians, we are selfish and self-serving. We don't know any other way to live. As I shared in the beginning pages of this book, that was how I lived my life before I became a Christian. I wanted what *I* wanted. I wanted to do what *I* wanted to do. I thought of only one person—*me!* And I served only one person—*me*.

But then the day I became a Christian through faith in Jesus Christ, I was overwhelmed (and still am to this day) that Jesus died for me. His death wiped away my sins and gave me new life—eternal life!—and a fresh start. I was "born again" (John 3:3)! I was "a new creation" (2 Corinthians 5:17) who had been given *new* life and a *new* heart.

And God's transforming grace and power was at work in me. I realized instantly that I owed a debt I could not pay—but I could, out of pure gratitude, serve my Lord to my dying breath. Oh, how I wanted to do just that! Gratitude is truly a great motivator for serving the Lord!

We serve like Jesus, our model—In our Savior, our Lord Jesus Christ, we have a perfect model of a life of service. How did Jesus live His life? In His own words, "I do not seek My own will but the will of the Father who sent Me" (John 5:30), and "My food is to do the will of Him who sent Me, and to finish His work" (4:34). And that will and "work," dear reader, was the work that accomplished our salvation from sin—the work of dying on the cross. Jesus explained His work and His mission with these words: "The Son of Man did not come to be served, but to *serve*, and to give His life a ransom for many" (Matthew 20:28). Thus, "Jesus...went about doing good" (Acts 10:38). And we as Christians are to "follow His steps" (1 Peter 2:21). Therefore...

> Go, labour on; spend and be spent—
> Thy joy to do the Father's will;
> It is the way the Master went;
> Should not the servant tread it still?[1]

We serve out our mandate—The Bible is very clear that every Christian, including you and me, is to serve the Lord. In fact, we are "spiritually gifted" to serve and expected to use those gifts in service. We are instructed that "the manifestation of the Spirit is given to each one for the profit of all" (1 Corinthians 12:7). "Through love" we are to "serve one another" (Galatians 5:13). Therefore, in obedience, we serve. It's our mandate!

And what is waiting for us on the other side of such obedience? The blessing of knowing we are serving God. The blessing of becoming more Christlike. The blessing of living out the highest form of leadership—that of humble service. And the blessing of demonstrating Christlikeness in the world: "The world cannot always understand one's profession of faith, but it can understand service."[2]

We serve as our ministry to others—The Bible informs us that the spiritual gifts that each Christian possesses are "for the profit of all" (1 Corinthians 12:7). Christians who are on the receiving end of the ministry of these gifts are benefited. Although Christians have been given a variety of spiritual gifts (verse 4), every one of them ministers to the members of the church, the body of Christ. When you discover, develop, and use your spiritual gift, others are edified, built up, encouraged, strengthened, comforted, helped, and matured in Christ.

There are many ways women serve others in the church—as many ways as there are gifts. My own personal goal is "to *teach* the Bible so that women's lives are changed." The reason I stated my personal desire in these words is because other women in my church were ministering their gift of teaching and my life had been marvelously changed as I drank in what they shared. I knew nothing about being a Christian or about spiritual gifts...or about teaching the Bible, for that matter. But I did know that somehow and in some way, the time and care and effort these women took to share with others was having a positive and powerful impact on my life as a new Christian woman, wife, and mother. And I thought and prayed, *Oh Lord, if I could do that for one more woman, if I could just pass on what I've learned, if I could just change one life the way these ladies have changed mine...how worthwhile that would be!*

And God has truly answered my prayer! I'll go into more specifics later, but for now, remember that your faithful service and the faithful use of your spiritual giftedness ministers to others more than you'll ever know. God planned it that way!

> *We serve the Lord. This truth attaches great dignity to our service, however seemingly small or menial.*

We serve our Master—It always helps me to know *why* I should do something, which is what we've been considering so far regarding our service in the body of Christ. But I also like to know *who* it is I am doing anything for. And in the case of spiritual service and ministry, the Bible tells us *Who* we are serving: "for you serve the Lord Christ" (Colossians 3:24). This truth attaches great dignity to our service, no matter how small or menial it may seem.

Serving as a Couple

As the subtitle of this books states, there are 12 things that really make a difference in your marriage that I've chosen to include in this book about being a wife after God's own heart. And serving the Lord as a couple is one of those "things." This may or may not be possible for you in your unique marital situation, but let's look at two couples after God's own heart who ministered together in serving others.

Meet Sarah and Abraham—Together Sarah and Abraham make up one of God's dynamic couples of faith. Each had a heart after God. Each loved God. Each followed God. Each trusted God. And each has been eternally honored by God for the faith exhibited in Him in situation after situation for year after year and decade after decade (Hebrews 11:8-19). How did this husband and wife serve the Lord as a couple?

Sarah and Abraham worked together as a team. One day when Abraham was resting in the door of his tent in the desert, he spied three men coming his way. He jumped up, ran to meet them, bowed before the men, invited them in, and offered a little water and a place to rest along with the promise of food…

…which is where Sarah came in! Abraham rushed into their tent, spouted out orders to Sarah to Quick! Make some bread cakes! He even gave her the recipe! Then off Abraham scurried, disappearing to take care of the meat for the meal they were jointly preparing for their guests. Together they pulled it off, and their mutual ministry of hospitality created a place of refuge and refreshment in a ruthless climate for their visitors (Genesis 18:1-8).

Just an afterword: The three "men" who stopped by Sarah and Abraham's tent for a little visit just happened to be "the Lord" and "two angels."[3] These heavenly visitors were on a two-fold mission. They had come to deliver a message to Sarah and Abraham that, after 25 years of waiting, they would finally have a child (Genesis 18:9-15). They had also come to deliver Abraham's nephew, Lot, out of the evil environment in Sodom and Gomorrah before the angels destroyed it (Genesis 19:1-29).

Pointing to the ministry of hospitality to others, instances like the kindness Sarah and Abraham served up to three desert travelers, the Bible says "do not forget to entertain strangers, for by so doing some have unwittingly entertained angels" (Hebrews 13:2)! When you minister to someone, you never know how far-reaching that service may be!

Meet Priscilla and Aquila—Here's an amazing couple who served the Lord together. In fact, throughout the New Testament there is a trail of shining examples of their team ministry. First, Priscilla and Aquila took in the apostle Paul and provided a home for him (Acts 18:1-3). Many scholars believe that Paul may have stayed with this fine couple for the entire year and a half he ministered in Corinth. Priscilla and Aquila also took aside the Jewish teacher Apollos and "explained to him the way of God more accurately," and then sent

> *"It is not the possession of extraordinary gifts that matter...but the dedication of what we have to the service of God."*

him on his way to a greater ministry as "he vigorously refuted the Jews publicly, showing from the Scriptures that Jesus is the Christ" (Acts 18:24-28).

Adding to their résumé of ministries, Paul later wrote that Priscilla and Aquila had been his "fellow workers in Christ Jesus, who risked their own necks" for his life (Romans 16:3-4). Paul also sent greetings to the church at Corinth from Aquila and Priscilla and "the church that is in their house" (1 Corinthians 16:19). Then, when the political and religious climate cooled down, Priscilla and Aquila returned to their roots in Rome and hosted another "house church" (Romans 16:5). Everywhere they went this admirable couple served the Lord.

Together Priscilla and Aquila worked as tentmakers, knew and shared the teachings of God's Word, opened their home, and encountered life-threatening persecution. What a couple! They were constantly on the move. But their eyes and ears, not to mention their hearts, were open to those in need. They were ready, willing, and able (at least with the little they had!) to serve the Lord any where, in any way, at any time, and at any cost. Jim and I have picked Priscilla and Aquila as our model of not only a marriage after God's own heart, but of a couple who together served the Lord heartily. Maybe you and your husband can do the same.

Abraham and Sarah, Priscilla and Aquila. Two couples after God's own heart...in two different time periods...in two different lands...ministering to two different kinds of people—one to the Lord Himself and His angels, and the other to the Lord's church and His servants Paul and Apollos. Yet each couple had a heart for God, a marriage that withstood the rigors of trials and time, a "home" that they opened up, along with their hearts, to others. In marriage and in ministry, each couple operated as an effective team, bringing twice the love, twice the strength, and twice the service to those in need. These two noble couples gave freely of their means and possessions in their ministries to others. They lived out this truth about serving the Lord: "It is not the possession of extraordinary gifts that makes extraordinary usefulness, but the dedication of what we have to the service of God."[4]

Principles for a Wife's Ministry

There are as many service-scenarios in a marriage as there are couples, but several principles for a wife's ministry apply in all circumstances. This set of principles will help you in your particular husband/wife situation. In my situation, my Jim has been in ministry for almost 30 years (which is a service-scenario in itself!). So we know how to serve the Lord together. But I want to quickly say that it was not always like this!

No, I remember all too well our "start-up" days as a Christian couple—days when we were trying to get the 12 issues we are addressing in this book into place...and serving the Lord was one of them. In our case, Jim wanted to serve the Lord, but I didn't...or didn't know how to. I remember, too, our first efforts at mutual ministry— learning how to use my home for the good of others, how to make it...and my heart...available to God. I remember discovering, with God's help, how to be willing to serve others whenever Jim phoned home to say there was someone who needed assistance or money or a place to stay.

How does a wife assist her husband in serving the Lord? And how does a wife serve the Lord if her husband is lagging behind? And how does a wife serve the Lord if her husband is not a Christian?

1. *Serve those at home first*—For decades I've had a personal motto I use when it comes to my service to others and to my church: "Don't give away to others what you have not first given away at home." This saying reminds me of my God-given priorities every day. I am to serve my husband and children, to give my love to those at home *first*...and then move on to share with others—not the other way around. I know how easy it is to get the order backward, and so do other women just like you and me. For instance...

Recently I talked to a woman who had resigned as the director of women's ministries at her church. Why? She said she withdrew from her position because her priorities were out of order. She told me that she found it much easier and more rewarding to minister to the women at church than to take care of the needs of her two preschoolers and her husband at home.

Another woman who served as a music and worship leader and soloist at one of my conferences left that conference deeply convicted of her wrong priorities. (In fact, she was on her way to a pay phone to call her husband and ask his forgiveness!) She told me afterward that when she said goodbye to her husband as she left home that morning to attend the "A Woman After God's Own Heart" seminar, she really meant the "goodbye." She had announced to him that she wouldn't be coming back—ever. Beloved, she went *home* from that seminar a *wife* after God's own heart!

In both cases these women were giving away to others what they were definitely not giving away at home. But I say of these two women, *Bravo!* for recognizing their wrong priorities and *Praise God!* for wanting to do the right thing! As a wife, you are to serve your husband first before any and all others. What's important is not what those at church think of you, but what those at *home* think of you. What's important is not that those at church are taken care of, but that those at *home* are tended to. That's a wife's job, a wife's priority, and a wife's privilege!

Dear wife, when the people and the place at home are taken care of, loved, served, and fussed over, it is *then* that we go over to the church and take care of and tend to others. That's what a wife after God's own heart does.

2. *Serve with your husband's blessing and support*—If and when you do desire to sign up for a ministry or volunteer to help in some way at the church, please—oh please—ask your husband first. Your relationship with your husband, your submission to his desires for your marriage and his leadership of the two of you as a couple, and your service to him is to be "as to the Lord" (Ephesians 5:22) and to be done "heartily, as to the Lord and not to men" (Colossians 3:23).

I personally make it a policy to never commit to anything or to take on any project without asking for Jim's input, thoughts, ideas, and approval. It's not because I'm afraid of my husband or see Jim as a parental figure. No, it's because I value the relationship and friendship we have as a couple *more than* I desire to do what I want to do. After all, if my time is involved in the ministry, that's Jim's time too. If money is involved, that's Jim's money too. If stress is involved (like the stress I incurred the first time I signed up to teach a women's Bible class), then that stress is bound to come Jim's way too.

It's like this. I want to serve the Lord, but I also want God's blessing on that service. And I believe that a mega-measure of God's blessing comes with my obedience to God's standards for me as a wife to honor my husband by giving preference to him (Romans 12:10), to esteem him as better than myself (Philippians 2:3), and to, as much as depends on me, live peaceably with my husband (Romans 12:18). Therefore I ask for Jim's opinion and approval on all things, including ministry opportunities. I don't ever want to find myself in a position of functioning in ministry (of all things!) without my husband's backing. So I serve *only* with my husband's blessing and support. Then I can serve with a free heart. Why? Because I know Jim's on board—and praying for me. Together we've released and designated some of my precious time and energy for ministry, which means it's a joint ministry. Sure, we evaluate afterward, but many times I make it through a ministry commitment only because I know in my heart that I have Jim's support.

And what's a wife to do if her husband says *no* (and, believe me, Jim has said *no* many times!)? If you are that wife, I say you should thank God. Your husband is key to helping you keep your priorities straight because his input can sound the alarm when things are out of balance. His direction is a way God guides you. So when my Jim says *no,* I personally thank God for a husband who leads and who speaks up. And then I decline the ministry opportunity without a bitter bone in my body. Following God's will that I follow my husband's leadership keeps me—and my service—in the center of God's will. *No* in an area of service can be God's will and direction as much as a *yes* can be.

3. *Serve however you can*—When Jim and I began going to church as a Christian couple, we didn't know anything about how to serve the Lord or about the Bible or about spiritual gifts. But with grateful hearts for our Savior, we knew we wanted to do something. So we did any and everything we could do! We washed dishes after socials. We set up chairs, took down chairs, stacked chairs, moved chairs for meetings. We put hymnals in the pews and vacuumed the sanctuary. We washed pots and pans during conferences. We greeted people coming to church services. We hosted a Bible study in our home. We drove senior citizens to church. We worked concession stands for the children's fair. We painted. We gardened. We helped complete the office ceilings during the remodeling of our church. On and on the list of our multi-faceted serving ministry went. We didn't need to have any special skills to do these wonderful ministries. We only needed to show up with a heart to serve.

Later, as we grew in our knowledge of God's Word, our ministries evolved. We took a counselor training course and began ministering in the prayer room after church services. We took an evangelistic outreach class and joined the visitation ministry. We took a Sunday school teacher training course and began assisting in children's classes. We took a discipleship training class and began ministering to others one on one. We took several Bible courses and began sharing in small group settings. And during all of the ministries and the taking of the classes and the growing spiritually steps, we used our home. Anyone and everyone was welcome there, whether local or from across the world!

But what if your husband doesn't want you to serve in these ways? Consider what you can do in your situation. I can't tell you how many women I know who bake cookies for ministry...from home, who fix meals for others...from home, who make phone calls to organize some ministry or check up on those who are home-bound...from home, who write letters and notes of encouragement...from home, who type lists of church information...from home, and who, of course, pray for others at church and around the world... from home. The ways to help and minister from home are unlimited—if you have a heart for serving the Lord!

All of this to say, my reading friend after God's own heart, serve however you can!

> Three things the Master asks of us,
> And we who serve Him here below
> And long to see His kingdom come
> May pray or give or go.

He needs them all—the open hand,
The willing feet, the praying heart,
To work together and to weave
A threefold cord that shall not part.[5]

Heart Response

And there's one more principle that's at the heart of everything...

Develop a servant's heart—As a woman after God's own heart, we—and every Christian!—can and should embrace the fact that every day of our God-given life is to be a time of glorious service. We are to be God's servant to all. We are to willingly serve everyone God allows to cross our path every day, beginning with our precious husbands. We are to mimic the Savior, who came to serve instead of to be served, and who went about doing good.

So I urge you to *pray!* Pray for a servant's heart every day—preferably first thing in the morning. Praying will remind you who you are, who you belong to, why you are here, and how God wants you to live your life. So, no matter what your marriage situation is like, boldly ask God for His love to serve your husband. Ask Him for His love to serve friends and foes, the familiar (your husband and children)...and the stranger. Ask God for greater compassion and for ears that hear and eyes that see where you can help. Ask for His tender mercies...and a heart for serving Him and the people He places in your path.

Little Things That Make a Big Difference

1. Pick one little thing to do at your church.

It can take a while to mature and prepare for some ministries. But there are a myriad of service and volunteer ministries you can do at your church that benefit multitudes. You can address and stuff envelopes, sanitize the nursery and its toys, vacuum the sanctuary, place items in the pews, bake a meal for a shut-in, greet visitors, assist a preschool teacher...and the list goes on and on. If you're not sure where to begin, ask someone in the church office. That someone will definitely know where the needs are! And sometimes those needs are "little things" that will make a big difference in your church being perceived as friendly and efficient.

2. Check your heart...and check your schedule.

This may sound strange since we are addressing our service to the Lord and His people. But it is easy for an eager Christian woman to overindulge in service...to the point of neglecting her marriage and family and home. Are your family members at home happy with the care and attention they are receiving? Is your husband fully (and I mean *fully!*) supportive of your involvement at church? Don't be like the woman who left home on a Saturday morning to lead the "worship" at an all-day seminar sponsored by her church—and who announced to her husband when she closed the door that she wasn't ever returning. Don't be like the wife and mother who found organizing and directing a full-blown ministry to the women at her church easier and more fulfilling than managing her home and caring for her husband and two little ones. Clearly these women had their priorities backward and were overindulging in ministry! So first do these two "little things"—check your calendar and check with your husband concerning your ministry involvement.

3. Agree with your husband on how to serve as a couple.

Few things are more rewarding for a Christian couple than serving the Lord *together!* Each of you brings so much to a couple's ministry. And you fill in each other's strengths and weaknesses when you team up to serve. For instance, perhaps your husband can lead or chair a ministry...and you can assist with the secretarial work for that ministry. Or if he needs to arrange an organizational meeting, you can volunteer to host the meeting in your home. If you both like people, you can sign up as greeters one Sunday a month. Do the two of you like to work with children? Then take on a class of little ones...together. How about helping with "the moving ministry"? You can cook a meal for an unsettled family while your husband helps move their furniture. Just be sure you both agree on how and how often you will serve. The list of ways the two of you can minister together is unending. It's as long as your hearts are big!

4. Serve in at least three ways.

A bit of information regarding serving others helped me get started down the road to ministry. Basically it points out three ministries that are not optional for a woman after God's own heart, but are commanded—serving, giving, and showing mercy. Here's how these ministries are explained:

> *Serving* (also sometimes called helps or ministering) is the basic ability to help other people, and there is no reason why every Christian cannot have and use this gift.

> *Showing mercy* is akin to the gift of ministering and involves succoring those who are sick or afflicted.

> *Giving* is the ability to distribute one's own money to others, and it is to be done with simplicity, which means with no thought of return or gain for oneself in any way.[6]

So what can...and will...you do this week to serve, show mercy, and give?

5. Pray for others.

Are you a stay-at-home woman? Do you have little ones at home? A job at home? Do you have a work schedule that doesn't allow you to be at church as much as you would like? Well, you can always pray. Ask your church for a list of weekly prayer requests. Also carry a special notebook to church to record the prayer requests shared by others. Then pray for those in your church and around the world. Remember, the effective fervent prayer of a praying *woman* accomplishes much (James 5:16)!

12

Reaching Out to Others

You shall be witnesses to Me
in Jerusalem, and in all Judea and Samaria,
and to the end of the earth.
ACTS 1:8

Throughout this book I have shared about becoming a Christian. For the first 28 years of my life I did not have a relationship with God through His Son, Jesus Christ. I was selfish, my life was hopeless, and I was clueless about being a wife, mother, and homemaker. My heart was definitely not filled with love, joy, peace, and patience! Instead I had a bleeding ulcer, chronic colitis, and exema up to my elbows! I was most miserable, and I'm sure Jim and my two daughters were, too.

But then something happened. In simple terms, someone reached out to me with the truth of the gospel of Jesus Christ. And because God had graciously prepared my heart, I received that truth, was born again, and God's grace and transforming power began working in my heart. From that very second, God put me on the path to becoming a woman after His own heart. And that direction affected my marriage to Jim as I also began growing into a wife after God's own heart.

But how did such a transformation happen? Again, the short answer is that someone reached out to me. In fact, God used a series of people to reach out to me—people who followed Jesus' words at the beginning of this chapter. Jesus told His followers then to "be witnesses to Me in Jerusalem, and in all Judea and Samaria, and to the end of the earth" (Acts 1:8), and His words still stand for you and me today. Only the locations have changed!

If you are a Christian, I'm sure you can recount the trail of people—of witnesses—God used to bring His truth to you. And now I want you to become a part of the trail of witnesses that God just might use in the lives of others to introduce them to the Savior. As we move through this chapter, keep in mind we are moving through *your* Jerusalem (those in your home), *your* Judea and Samaria (those in your neighborhood and your family), and on to the end of the earth (the world)!

Reaching Out to Your Husband

The person closest to any wife is her own dear husband. And many Christian wives are married to men who are not believers in Christ. What advice does God give to such a wife?

If this describes your marital situation, these words possess the pure wisdom of God: "Wives, likewise, be submissive to your own husbands, that even if some do not obey the word, they, without a word, may be won by the conduct of their wives, when they observe your chaste conduct" (1 Peter 3:1-2). Here the apostle Peter counsels all Christian wives to "be submissive to your own husbands."

But then Peter addresses the wife who is married to a husband who does "not obey the word." This is a husband who is a non-Christian. How do you reach out to such a husband? God is very clear: You are to, "without a word," live out your Christianity by your "conduct." This doesn't mean you can never speak or speak up. But it does mean you are not to preach, lecture, harass, goad, or nag. Instead God wants your *life* to send a loud message from Him to your husband's heart. And God chooses to—and is able to!—deliver that message through your reverent and respectful behavior as a wife. Living a loving life preaches a louder and lovelier message than your lips could ever proclaim!

> *Living a lovely life preaches a louder and lovelier message than your lips could ever proclaim.*

Just a personal note here... In the early days of my marriage to Jim, we were "unequally yoked"...only in our case, Jim was the believer and I was the unbeliever. I can well imagine the tightrope an unequally yoked woman walks because I dished out plenty of hostility, put-downs, and scorn to Jim about his beliefs in Jesus Christ. I lived out this truth in the Bible: "But the natural man does not receive the things of the Spirit of God, for they are foolishness to him; nor can he know them, because they are spiritually discerned" (1 Corinthians 2:14). But Jim was so very patient, kind, forgiving, and loving. It's hard to resist such Christlike behavior! Jim was a major link in the chain God forged to draw me to Himself. I pray that you will be just such a link in the life of your husband!

In addition to godly behavior, you can—and should!—pray. "The effective, fervent prayer of a righteous [wife] avails much" (James 5:16)! Who knows what your godly conduct and your faithful prayers can, by God's grace, accomplish in your husband's heart?

Reaching Out to Your Children

Following on the heels of your love for your dear husband are your precious children, if you have them. Your job assignment from God is to reach out to them with the life-saving message of Jesus Christ. These flesh-and-blood gifts from God are entrusted to you as a woman and a mother after God's own heart, and God expects you to teach, instruct, and train your children for Him and His purposes. And these roles are not optional. No, they are commanded by God:

> These words which I command you today shall
> be in your heart. You shall teach them diligently
> to your children (Deuteronomy 6:6-7).

> Train up a child in the way he should go
> (Proverbs 22:6).

> Bring them up in the training and admonition of
> the Lord (Ephesians 6:4).

Fellow mother, we are to give our all each and every day to obey these commands and do our part to lead our little (and big!) ones to the knowledge of God and His Son, Jesus Christ. No price can be put on a soul, especially those of our nearest and dearest—our children! As a mom, I found that I needed to make a fresh commitment to God daily as a personal reminder of the importance of reaching out to my flock of children, no matter what age they were at the time. If I didn't have this fresh, daily reminder, I tended to let things slide, to take the easy road, to do as little as possible, to lose sight of my mission as a *Christian* mother. So as a dedicated Christian mother, you must see to it that you not only discipline and train your children but that you...

> ...read the Bible regularly to them,

> ...study the lives of God's great heroes of the faith
> with them,

> ...have daily devotions with them,

> ...help to hide God's Word in their hearts,

> ...take them to church, Sunday school, and church
> activities,

> ...speak of the Lord continually to them,

...point the events of their lives to biblical truth,

...pray for and with them at bedtime,

...teach them about Jesus, and

...freely and frequently share God's plan of salvation.

And, of course, as a passionate and devoted mother, you must pray for them. Remember James 5:16? "The effective, fervent prayer of a righteous [mother] avails much." Who knows what your godly conduct, your dedicated teaching, and your faithful prayers can, by God's grace, accomplish in your children's hearts, no matter how young or old they are?

Reaching Out to Your Neighbors

Next come your neighbors. They may not be as close to you emotionally as your family members are, but you live near them day-in, day-out. That means you probably see your neighbors more often than you see your own extended family. And, as a wise proverb reminds us, "Better is a neighbor nearby than a brother far away" (Proverbs 27:10). In other words, when you have a need or an emergency, your neighbor is there to turn to for help—not your relatives!

Jesus has something to say about neighbors. Quoting from the Old Testament Law of Moses, He said that as a woman after God's own heart, you are to "love the LORD your God with all your heart, with all your soul, and with all your mind" and "love your neighbor as yourself" (Matthew 22:37 and 39).

So, as a wise woman who wants to reach out to your neighbors, you must first have a heart full of love for them. And I've always found that prayer is how such a heart and such a love is cultivated. That's how Jim and I approached our neighbors and neighborhood. We picked one day each week to pray specifically for our neighbors. We listed each family on a special prayer page, along with their children's names. Then, as we spent time in the yard or passed one another getting in and out of the car, we would take a minute (no matter how busy or rushed we were!) to greet our neighbors by name, to be friendly, and to find out something else about their lives...which was noted on their personal prayer pages. Amazingly, as we prayed regularly for our neighbors, they came to have a place in our hearts...and in our lives! Prayer entwined our lives with theirs. Prayer turned strangers into loved ones!

Make it a project to pray and ask God to help you think of as many ways as you can to help your neighbors, to have them in to your home and over for dinner. As you live out your Christianity before their eyes, you can be sure religion will come up. As your neighbors see you leave

> *A heart filled with God's love will smooth the way for reaching out.*

for church each week, your interest in church is guaranteed to come up! And remember, it doesn't matter if they understand you and your Christianity. Just be a friend. Keep opening your door...and your heart. Keep serving, loving, helping, befriending. And by all means, keep asking if they would like to go to church with you or go to a choir concert or church picnic, your women's Bible study, an exercise group, or a quilting class at church. Ask if their children would like to go to your church's organized children's ministry.

In these ways—and more!—friendships are built. Then, as you already know, you can talk to a friend about anything...including Jesus Christ!

Reaching Out to Your Family

Reaching out with the gospel message of Jesus Christ to extended family members can definitely be a touchy area. But the good news is that it is nothing that God cannot enable you to handle graciously and in a Christlike manner. A heart filled with God's love will smooth the way for reaching out to family—both your relatives and those of your husband! (Please revisit Chapter 8, "Extending Love to Family"!) Hopefully you've already been working on your love for, acceptance of, and responsibility toward these God-given family members.

But your goal with family should always be, as the scripture verse for Chapter 8 states, to, "if it is possible, as much as depends on *you*, live peaceably with all men" (Romans 12:18). As a Christian, you have the living Christ living in you to help you to live out the part that depends on you (Colossians 1:27). You have God's fruit of the Spirit at work in you—His love, His joy, His peace, His patience, His self-control to aid you (Galatians 5:22-23). Therefore, from your end of family relationships, you *can* get along, reach out in love, and come to their aid with the help and service and understanding needed. So the issue and the hard question then becomes, Do you want to?

I know some family members can be a challenge. They may even want nothing to do with you. And when that's the case (as in any and all cases!), you pray! God is well able to soften hard hearts as you lift up your sincere prayers on their behalf. My prayer principles stand for difficult family members: *You cannot hate the person you are praying for* and *You cannot neglect the person you are praying for.* Try it! You'll find out firsthand that these are true. Not only does prayer change family members—prayer changes *you*!

So think through the family members God has given you. In fact, make a list in your prayer notebook. Then make it a point to find out birthdates for everyone on your list...and send something each year, no matter what! Find out anniversary dates too...and send something annually, no matter what! Collect email addresses...and send a regular update and inquiry, no matter what! Reach out, stay in touch, seek to shore up broken relationships and better those you enjoy. Again, members of your own family can become your best friends...and with a friend you can talk about anything—including Jesus Christ!

Reaching Out to the World

We've now covered the many people who make up your daily life—your husband, children, family, and your neighbors. (And space doesn't even allow us to address reaching out to those wonderful people at your workplace!) So who's left? Why, the whole world! But take cheer! You can be a part of extending the truth about Christ and His love to those in the world...beginning right at your own church.

I've already mentioned that my Jim served for some 25 years as a pastor and Bible teacher. In fact, Jim was Pastor of Evangelism at our former church. That means we served for many years in our church's outreach ministries. What kind of ministries? We've both been involved in the church's prayer room where people came for help, guidance...and in search of a relationship with God. We've put in time at the church's information booth where visitors came for information and directions to classrooms...as well as to God! And the list goes on. Jim and I have both participated in the visitation ministry. We've both reached out in jails, at missions for the homeless, and at shelters and halfway houses. We've "manned" the hotline at church, participated in college campus and street ministries. We've gone on short-term missions trips together and even served as missionaries in Singapore.

Reaching Out...Carefully!

Such opportunities for reaching out to others exist through your church, too. But...*be careful!* As a wife after God's own heart, you must always go right back to the "Principles for a Wife's Ministry" shared in the previous chapter. Those principles are:

#1. Serve those at home first.

#2. Serve with your husband's blessing and support.

#3. Serve however you can.

If your husband doesn't want to be involved, or if he wants you to be less involved, or if he objects to your involvement, go very slowly, very carefully, and very wisely. When it comes to your spiritual ministry and reaching out to others through your church, you want to, once again, serve with your husband's blessing and support (#2). You must also remember that you don't live at the church. No, you live in a home where you have a husband to serve (#1), love, care for, spoil, pamper, and reach out to if he's not a Christian.

Of course, the ideal scenario is to serve in an outreach ministry together with your husband. But the truth is that not many women get to live out this ideal. If this is your situation, and if your heart is willing to please your husband (1 Corinthians 7:34), then, believe me, there are still countless ways that you can reach out to others. So, rather than be bitter, put your trust in God and thank Him that He is in control of the circumstances of your marriage. Then pray and make it a personal project to see how many ways you can reach out from home (#3)...while you are honoring your husband's wishes. God will bless and honor you for that because honoring your husband is what a wife after God's own heart does (Ephesians 5:22 and 33)!

Heart Response

And now, dear friend and devoted-to-your-dear-husband wife, after traveling the road together through this book about being God's kind of wife, I want to reach out to *you!* It just occurred to me that I know nothing about your personal relationship with God. I've assumed a few things about you along the way simply because you have chosen to read this book with its lofty and hopeful title. I've assumed that...

...perhaps you are reading this volume because you were looking for help in your relationship with your husband or ways to better your marriage. If so, *bravo!* I hope and pray that the truths presented from the Bible, my personal insights, and the little things that make a big difference have indeed made a b-i-g difference! Or,

...perhaps a friend reached out and invited you to a Bible study and this is the book the women chose to use. Again, *well done!* for going to the study...and for completing the book! Or,

...perhaps your couples' Sunday school class is using this book (along with my husband's book for the men, *A Husband After God's Own Heart*)[1] and you and your husband joined the group. I say to you, *you are blessed!* What a blessing to go through these areas of your marriage together! How I pray your marriage has been enriched!

There's no doubt that this is a practical book. But I'm sure you also picked up on the more major theme threaded throughout the book—that of being *God's* kind of wife, of being a woman and a wife after *God's* own heart. You see, this book is also a spiritual book. So, as our joint journey ends and we part ways, I want to reach out to you. I believe you probably fall into one of these categories of women and wives:

—You are a woman after God's own heart and have embraced Jesus Christ as Lord. If so, I trust that after reading the truths in this book your faith in God has been built up, your dedication to following God's rules for your marriage has been kicked up a notch, and your commitment to be God's kind of wife has been firmed up. To you I say, *Keep on keeping on!* Keep on following God's plan for you as a wife. And by all means, keep on growing in the Lord! Or,

—You desire to be a woman after God's own heart, but you are unsure of your relationship with God through Jesus Christ. You like what you've been reading and desire to follow after God with your whole heart, but you're not sure you are a child of God. To you I say, *Come to the cross!* For you I share this acrostic that presents the truths of Jesus Christ's death. It is a statement of who Jesus Christ is and what His death on the cross accomplished in the plan of God. I am also sharing a prayer that might guide your heart to the right words for receiving Jesus Christ into your heart and life by faith.

C-hrist, God-in-flesh, gave His life (Philippians 2:8) as a

R-ansom, a payment, for our sins (Matthew 20:28),

O-ffering up His life as a sinless sacrifice (Hebrews 10:14),

S-uffering unto death (Hebrews 12:2) to secure our

S-alvation from sin and death (Colossians 2:13-14).[2]

A Prayer from My Heart

Jesus, I want to accept You as my personal Savior. Please come into my life and help me obey You from this day forward. I know I am a sinner, but I want to repent of my sins and turn and follow You. I believe You died on the cross for my sins and rose again victorious over the power of sin and death. I thank You with all my heart! Amen.

So now, my beloved friend, I leave you with one question. Have you embraced the Christ of the cross as your Savior? If not, know that I am praying for you to do so. Becoming a child of God will truly make *all* the difference in the world in every part of your life—including your marriage! And if so, reach out to others with God's message of the cross as you travel the path of life as a woman and a wife after God's own heart!

Little Things That Make a Big Difference

1. Invite your friends and neighbors to a Bible study.

Are you unsure about how to witness to people? Are you uncomfortable sharing with others? You can always introduce your friends and neighbors to Christianity by taking them with you to a Bible study. Your women's study and your couples' study are great places to take the women you know and the couples on your block. Simply reach out and invite them! Each time you begin a new study, pick up extra flyers to give to your associates, neighbors, friends, and the other moms at school along with a fresh invitation to join you. Your friendliness and enthusiasm for your group study just might encourage people to come along and take a look for themselves. Then...who knows what might happen!

2. Participate in activities with your friends and neighbors.

When it comes to reaching out to others, establish a general policy of saying *yes* to your neighbors when they invite you to do something (...with your husband's approval, of course!). Make it a point to go to as many Tupperware, Pampered Chef, or Avon parties as possible that are hosted by your unbelieving neighbors, co-workers, and school acquaintances. If these wonderful people invite you to a backyard barbeque, go! If someone's child is having a birthday, move heaven and earth to participate. If someone's daughter is getting married, do everything in your power to attend the wedding. If your neighbor's husband is in a baseball playoff, throw on a pair of jeans and you and your husband try to be there. Attempt to join your neighbors and associates in their endeavors as often as you can. They need to know that you are vitally interested in them. Don't be so wrapped up in your church that you are perceived as distant or aloof—as people who could care less about neighbors' and friends' lives...and souls.

3. Open your home.

Never underestimate the power of a Christian home! As a believer, "you are the light of the world." Therefore your home is like "a city that is set on a hill" (Matthew 5:14). It is full of light, ablaze with the glory of God at work in you and in your home. Therefore, fling wide the doors of your wonderful home. Like the wise woman in Proverbs 9, call to those who need the truth, "Turn in here!...Come, eat of my bread" (verses 4-5). If a neighbor is going through a rough time, have her over for coffee. If a new family moves in, have them come for a chili supper. Consider an open house every year for you and/or your husband's co-workers. Have the school moms to your house for coffee cake and a gab session. Hospitality is a marvelous gift you can give to others and a wonderful way to make friends. And with a friend, you can talk about anything—including Jesus Christ.

4. Give a book or a Christian tract.

You may be unsure about how to witness or you may be uncomfortable sharing with others, but you can always introduce your friends and neighbors to Christianity by giving them a book or a tract. You do the giving, and then stand back and see how God chooses to use it in the lives of others. If a particular Christian book has helped you improve your marriage, share the good news! Give the book to other wives. If a book on biblical child-raising principles has given you greater confidence in your parenting, share the good news! Give the book to other mothers. And how about housework? Has a book by a Christian homemaker shown you better methods and quicker ways to take care of the place where you live? Then share the good news! Give the book to other struggling home managers. Have a generous, thoughtful heart. Speak up when something helps you as a woman. Then put a book or a tract into the hands of those who so need the help the Bible and the Savior can give them!

5. Pray for your unbelieving friends and acquaintances.

The greatest way to "love your neighbors" is to pray for them. This is also the greatest way to develop a heart of compassion for your unbelieving friends and neighbors. As you faithfully bring their need for the Savior and the difficulties of their lives before God through prayer, your heart becomes mightily involved. Your "care quotient" goes up as you invest your time and spiritual energy in praying for them. Keep a prayer list. Let others know you are praying for them. Check up regularly on the issues in their lives.

Notes

Chapter 1: Growing in the Lord

1. Neil S. Wilson, ed., *The Handbook of Life Application* (Wheaton, IL: Tyndale House Publishers, 1992), pp. 270-71.
2. Mark Porter, *The Time of Your Life* (Wheaton, IL: Victor Books, 1983), p. 114.

Chapter 2: Working as a Team

1. Charles F. Pfeiffer and Everett F. Harrison, eds., *The Wycliffe Bible Commentary* (Chicago: Moody Press, 1973), p. 5.
2. Ephesians 5:22; Colossians 3:18; and 1 Peter 3:1.
3. For a more in-depth discussion of these and other problems in marriage, please see Elyse Fitzpatrick and Carol Cornish, gen. eds., *Women Helping Women* (Eugene, OR: Harvest House Publishers, 1997).
4. John MacArthur, *The MacArthur Study Bible* (Nashville: Word Publishing, 1997), p. 1738.
5. Pfeiffer and Harrison, eds., *Wycliffe Bible Commentary*, p. 5.

Chapter 3: Learning to Communicate

1. The Living Bible.
2. Sid Buzzell, gen. ed., *The Leadership Bible* (Grand Rapids, MI: Zondervan Publishing House, 1998), p. 742.
3. Walter quoted in Eleanor L. Doan, *The Speaker's Sourcebook* (Grand Rapids, MI: Zondervan Publishing House, 1977), p. 298.
4. Ellen Fein and Sherrie Schneider, *The Rules for Marriage* (New York: Warner Books, Inc., 2001), pp. 83-85.

Chapter 4: Enjoying Intimacy

1. The Living Bible.
2. MacArthur, *MacArthur Study Bible*, p. 19.
3. Pfeiffer and Harrison, eds., *Wycliffe Bible Commentary*, p. 6.
4. MacArthur, *MacArthur Study Bible*, p. 1944.
5. Willard Harley in Alice Gray, *Lists to Live By*, The First Collection (Sisters, OR: Multnomah Publishers, 1999), p. 122.
6. Claudia and David Arp in Alice Gray, *Lists to Live By*, p. 137.

Chapter 5: Managing Your Money
1. 1 Corinthians 16:1-2; 2 Corinthians 9:5-7.
2. Elizabeth George, *Beautiful in God's Eyes—The Treasures of the Proverbs 31 Woman* (Eugene, OR: Harvest House Publishers, 1998).
3. Alice Gray, *Lists to Live By for Every Married Couple* (Sisters, OR: Multnomah Publishers, 2001), pp. 30-31.

Chapter 6: Keeping Up the Home
1. Carol Meyers, Toni Craven, and Ross S. Kraemer, *Women in Scripture* (Grand Rapids, MI: William B. Eerdmans Publishing Company, 2001), p. 306. The four other references referred to are Genesis 24:28; Ruth 1:8; Song of Solomon 3:4; 8:2.
2. Robert Jamieson, A.R. Fausset, and David Brown, *Commentary on the Whole Bible* (Grand Rapids, MI: Zondervan Publishing House, 1973), p. 466.
3. Curtis Vaughan, *The Old Testament Books of Poetry from 26 Translations,* quoting translations by Ronald Knox and Kenneth Taylor (Grand Rapids, MI: Zondervan Bible Publishers, 1973), p. 632.
4. Jamieson, Fausset, and Brown, *Commentary on the Whole Bible,* p. 1387.
5. Ibid.
6. Vaughan, *Old Testament Books of Poetry,* quoting translation by James Moffatt, p. 530.
7. Pfeiffer and Harrison, eds., *Wycliffe Bible Commentary,* p. 1394.
8. "Where Shall I Work Today," cited in V. Raymond Edman, *Disciplines of Life* (Minneapolis: World Wide Publications, 1948), p. 209.
9. Frank S. Mead, *12,000 Religious Quotations,* quoting James Hamilton (Grand Rapids, MI: Baker Book House, 2000), p. 230.
10. For additional help in creating a master plan for your home, visit www.flylady.net.

Chapter 7: Raising Your Children
1. Mead, *12,000 Religious Quotations,* quoting Samuel Taylor Coleridge, p. 338.

Chapter 8: Extending Love to Family
1. Cited in Edith L.Doan, *The Speaker's Sourcebook,* (Grand Rapids, MI: Zondervan Publishing House, 1977), p. 169. The author of the poem is unknown.

Chapter 9: Tending Your Career
1. Author unknown, cited in Edith L. Doan, *The Speaker's Sourcebook,* p. 282.
2. Mead, *12,000 Religious Quotations,* quoting Helen Hunt Jackson, p. 230.
3. George, *Beautiful in God's Eyes.*
4. Roy B. Zuck quoting F.B. Meyer in *The Speaking Quote Book* (Grand Rapids, MI: Kregel Publications, 1997), p. 409.

Chapter 10: Making Time for Fun
1. Elizabeth George, *Loving God with All Your Mind* (Eugene, OR: Harvest House Publishers, 1994).
2. See www.coloradohealthnet.org/depression, 3/11/99.
3. Ibid.
4. Derek Kidner, *The Proverbs* (Downers Grove, IL: InterVarsity Press, 1973), p. 114.

Chapter 11: Serving the Lord
1. Horatius Bonar.
2. Mead, *12,000 Religious Quotations,* quoting Ian MacLaren, p. 404.
3. Genesis 18:13-14,22; 19:1.
4. Mead, *12,000 Religious Quotations,* quoting Frederick Willaim Robertson, p. 404.
5. Author unknown, cited in Edith L. Doan, *The Speaker's Sourcebook,* p. 223.
6. Charles Caldwell Ryrie, *Balancing the Christian Life* (Chicago: Moody Press, 1969), pp. 96-97.

Chapter 12: Reaching Out to Others
1. Jim George, *A Husband After God's Own Heart* (Eugene, OR: Harvest House Publishers, 2004).
2. Elizabeth George in Rob Holt, *What the Cross Means to Me* (Eugene, OR: Harvest House Publishers, 2002), p. 27.

$\mathcal{I}$f you've benefited from *A Wife After God's Own Heart*, you'll want the companion volume

A Wife After God's Own Heart

Growth and Study Guide

This guide offers thought-provoking questions, reflective studies, and personal applications that will enrich your life.

This growth and study guide is perfect for both personal and group use.

$\mathcal{D}$ouble the benefits of *A Wife After God's Own Heart*, by giving your husband the companion volume

A Husband After God's Own Heart

This book by Jim George is rich with practical insights and guidance that will bring greater mutual love, friendship, romance, and happiness to your marriage.

Books by Jim and Elizabeth George are available at your local Christian bookstore or can be ordered from:

Jim and Elizabeth George Ministries
P.O. Box 2879
Belfair, WA 98528
Toll-free fax/phone: 1-800-542-4611
www.jimgeorge.com

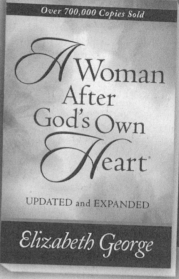

A Woman After God's Own Heart® Study Series

BIBLE STUDIES FOR BUSY WOMEN

"God wrote the Bible to change hearts and lives. Every study in this series is written with that in mind—and is specially focused on helping Christian women know how God desires for them to live."

—Elizabeth George

Sharing wisdom gleaned from more than 20 years as a women's Bible study teacher, Elizabeth has prepared insightful lessons that can be completed in 15 to 20 minutes per day. Each lesson includes thought-provoking questions and insights, Bible study tips, instructions for leading a discussion group, and a "heart response" section to make the Bible passage more personal.

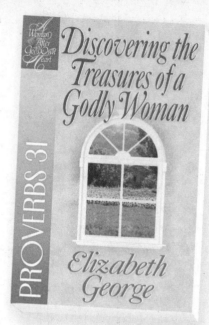

Proverbs 31 0-7369-0818-8

Philippians 0-7369-0289-9

1 Peter 0-7369-0290-2

1 Timothy 0-7369-0665-7

Judges/Ruth 0-7369-0498-0

Esther 0-7369-0489-1

James 0-7369-0490-5

Life of Mary 0-7369-0300-3

Life of Sarah 0-7369-0301-1

Books by Elizabeth George

- Beautiful in God's Eyes
- Life Management for Busy Women
- Loving God with All Your Mind
- A Mom After God's Own Heart
- Powerful Promises for Every Woman
- The Remarkable Women of the Bible
- Small Changes for a Better Life
- A Wife After God's Own Heart
- A Woman After God's Own Heart®
- A Woman After God's Own Heart® Deluxe Edition
- A Woman's Call to Prayer
- A Woman's High Calling
- A Woman's Walk with God
- A Young Woman After God's Own Heart
- A Young Woman's Call to Prayer
- A Young Woman's Walk with God

Children's Books

- God's Wisdom for Little Girls
- A Little Girl After God's Own Heart

Study Guides

- Beautiful in God's Eyes Growth & Study Guide
- Life Management for Busy Women Growth & Study Guide
- Loving God with All Your Mind Growth & Study Guide
- A Mom After God's Own Heart Growth & Study Guide
- The Remarkable Women of the Bible Growth & Study Guide
- Small Changes for a Better Life Growth & Study Guide
- A Wife After God's Own Heart Growth & Study Guide
- A Woman After God's Own Heart® Growth & Study Guide
- A Woman's Call to Prayer Growth & Study Guide
- A Woman's High Calling Growth & Study Guide
- A Woman's Walk with God Growth & Study Guide

Books by Jim & Elizabeth George

- God Loves His Precious Children
- God's Wisdom for Little Boys

Books by Jim George

- The Bare Bones Bible Handbook
- God's Man of Influence
- A Husband After God's Own Heart
- A Man After God's Own Heart
- The Remarkable Prayers of the Bible
- The Remarkable Prayers of the Bible Growth & Study Guide
- What God Wants to Do for You
- A Young Man After God's Own Heart